OLDEST
TWIN CITIES

A GUIDE TO HISTORIC TREASURES

JULIE JO SEVERSON

REEDY PRESS

Copyright © 2023

All rights reserved.

Reedy Press

PO Box 5131

St. Louis, MO 63139

www.reedypress.com

We (the publisher and the author) have done our best to provide the most accurate information available when this book was completed. However, we make no warranty, guarantee, or promise about the accuracy, completeness, or currency of the information provided, and we expressly disclaim all warranties, expressed or implied. Please note that attractions, company names, addresses, websites, and phone numbers are subject to change or closure, and this is outside of our control. We are not responsible for any loss, damage, injury, or inconvenience that may occur due to the use of this book.

Library of Congress Control Number: 2022949149

ISBN: 9781681064345

Cover Design: Jill Halpin

Book Design: Linda Eckels

All photos are by Julie Jo Severson unless otherwise stated.

Printed in the United States of America

23 24 25 26 27 5 4 3 2 1

TABLE OF CONTENTS

Acknowledgments.............. v

Introduction vi

MINNEAPOLIS

Oldest Family Steakhouse 2

Oldest Northside Theater 4

Oldest Neighborhood 6

Oldest Street 8

Oldest Continuous
   Church.............................. 10

Oldest Frame House............ 12

Oldest Island Venue............. 14

Oldest Train Hub.................. 16

Oldest Flour Mill Site 18

Oldest Bridge Relics............. 20

Oldest Northloop Bar.......... 22

Oldest Skyscraper................. 24

Oldest Downtown Bar 26

Oldest Improv Company.... 28

Oldest Basilica in
   America............................. 30

Oldest Nicollet Mall Art 32

Oldest "Best Bar"................. 34

Oldest American
   Indian Center................... 36

Oldest Library....................... 38

Oldest Washburn-Fair
   Oaks Mansion.................. 40

Oldest Food Co-Op............42

Oldest Sci-Fi Bookstore 44

Oldest Hiking Trail 46

Oldest Preservation 48

Oldest Cemetery 50

Oldest Nordic Center 52

Oldest Bowling Alley...........54

Oldest Black-Owned
   Business.............................56

Oldest Rose Garden............58

ST. PAUL

Oldest State Building...........62

Oldest Natural Spring.........64

Oldest Jewish Deli...............66

Oldest Golf Course 68

Oldest Carousel 70

Oldest State Fair Ride 72

Oldest University.................74

Oldest Park Shelter..............76

Oldest Used Bookstore........78

Oldest Black Church...........80

Oldest Synagogue................82

Oldest "New" Supper
   Club...................................84

Oldest Curling Roots...........86

Oldest Outdoor
   Sculpture 88

Oldest Czech-Slovak Hall...90

Oldest Lager Saloon............92

Oldest Firehouse.................. 94

Oldest Neighborhood 96

Oldest Italian Market........... 98

Oldest Cultural
    Institution 100

Oldest Public Square 102

Oldest Downtown
    Building.......................... 104

Oldest Railcar Diner.......... 106

Oldest Art Museum 108

Oldest Theater Space 110

Oldest Sporting Club......... 112

Oldest Mexican Eatery...... 114

Oldest Cited Cave 116

Oldest Brewery Reborn 118

Oldest Family Italian
    Restaurant 120

Oldest Roundhouse........... 122

Oldest Cemetery 124

TWIN CITIES SUBURBS & BEYOND

Oldest Pro Theater 128

Oldest Dugout Canoe 130

Oldest Magic Shop............. 132

Oldest Music Store............. 134

Oldest Suburb 136

Oldest Private Home 138

Oldest Church in State 140

Oldest Blufftop
    Landmark 142

Oldest Grain Elevator........ 144

Oldest Lilac Way Relics..... 146

Oldest Public
    Wildflower Garden 148

Oldest Bar in State.............. 150

Oldest Skate Shop.............. 152

Oldest Lutheran Church... 154

Oldest General Store.......... 156

Oldest Courthouse............. 158

Oldest Ice Cream Shop 160

Oldest Winery.................... 162

Oldest Hotel 164

Oldest Covered Bridge...... 166

Oldest Observatory............ 168

Oldest Wool Mill............... 170

Oldest Continuous
    Brewery 172

Oldest Savu Sauna.............. 174

Sources 176

Index...............................183

ACKNOWLEDGMENTS

Eternal thanks to my parents, Diane and Bob Martinka, who passed away in 2020 and 2022, respectively. With eyes for beauty in all that's humble and enduring, they fostered in me a deep appreciation for unsung gems and stories that bind the generations together.

Much gratitude to my husband, Mike, and our grown-up children, Audrey, Caleb, and Amanda, for their support, patience, and levity. They know more than anyone what a true labor of love this book project has been for me.

Many thanks to the superheroes at Reedy Press. From *Secret Twin Cities* to *Oldest Twin Cities*, this has been a journey of infinite discovery that I don't take for granted.

None of this would've come to fruition without my longtime participation in the Twin Cities Writing Studio at ModernWell, a vibrant network of inspiring women, founded by Julie Burton and Nina Badzin. They've nudged and cheered this Minnesota girl way outside her comfort zone.

While researching and writing this book, I've relied on numerous resources. I'm especially indebted to curators of immense archives available through the Minnesota Historical Society, Minnesota Humanities Center, Hennepin History Museum, Ramsey County Historical Society, and the Hennepin County Library System. I also owe a mammoth thank you to several dozen business owners, general managers, museum directors, preservationists, and local historians. Despite countless other priorities, they kindly returned my calls, replied to my emails, gave me tours, agreed to impromptu interviews, and reviewed my drafts. These hardworking folks have renewed my faith in humanity and the Twin Cities community.

INTRODUCTION

When many of us are sensing a loss of community in this changing world, it can be good for the soul to experience those local places that transcend generations and offer continuity: An old-timey neighborhood deli. A vintage theater. An ancient landscape. A creaky-floored general store that sells homemade peach pies at the back counter. Learning about their storied legacies can deepen not only our reverence for bygone days but also our sense of place in the present.

Oldest Twin Cities turns back the pages of time through both legendary and little-known treasures that have endured wars, exploitation, the Great Depression, discrimination, fires, urban renewal, an unprecedented pandemic, and civil uprising. But the real stories are the people involved who've dreamed, hoped, struggled, sacrificed, made memories, and persevered.

First, there are Minnesota's Native American residents who've been stewards of this land for thousands of years. Minnesota is a word derived from the Dakota phrase *Mni Sóta Makoce*, which translates to "land where the waters reflect the clouds." Their roots here remain strong, but their history and the tragic erosion of their culture have often been absent from the dominant narrative.

Then came the surge of European and American explorers, fur traders, soldiers, pioneers, and colonists in search of land and economic opportunities, followed by waves of immigrants and war refugees from across the globe seeking to make Minnesota their home. Now the descendants of all groups carry the torch while navigating unsettling times.

Today, over half of Minnesota's population lives in the seven-county Twin Cities metropolitan area. At the heart of it are, of course, Minneapolis and St. Paul, centered around the confluence of the Mississippi, Minnesota, and St. Croix Rivers. It can be a bit of a struggle to describe where the "twins" begin and end, but they are independent municipalities with defined borders and their own unique characters.

St. Paul, our capital city, once a muddy river frontier town that became a transcontinental center for railroading (and for a time, a haven for gangsters), maintains a historic ambience. Meanwhile, Minneapolis, which grew up around St. Anthony Falls while becoming an epicenter for lumber and grain milling, has more of a sprawling big-city feel. But wherever you stand in the Twin Cities area, history is resonating.

I'm an observer, writer, editor, day-tripper, and deeply rooted Minnesotan who believes that when it comes to the well-being of a community and its residents, a feeling of connectedness to the places and stories that make our region distinct matters. The 85 vignettes in the pages ahead are mere glimpses of extensive histories. It's the nature of this type of book to provide concise descriptions, but brevity can't begin to do these age-old marvels justice. I can only hope that shining a light on these events and places might help rekindle an appreciation for the Twin Cities' rich, complex heritage and the good things going on all around us.

Find links to custom Google Maps for both *Oldest Twin Cities* and *Secret Twin Cities* at www.SecretTwinCities.com.

MINNEAPOLIS

View of Minneapolis's Stone Arch Bridge from the I-35W Bridge Collapse Remembrance Garden Memorial across from Gold Medal Park. Built from 1881 to 1883 by railroad baron James J. Hill, the Stone Arch Bridge, featuring 23 arches, is the second oldest bridge on the Mississippi River.

1933

OLDEST FAMILY STEAKHOUSE

JAX BAR AND CAFE

1928 NE University Ave., Mpls. 55418

There are few local restaurants dripping with as much character and nostalgia as Jax Cafe, a Northeast "Nordeast" Minneapolis landmark, operated by the Kozlak family for three generations. For some, Jax is where they learned to crack a lobster. For others, it's where they proposed to the love of their life, celebrated milestones, or gathered for annual family holiday brunches.

Besides the steak and seafood, it's the hospitality and quirky touches that have kept people coming back for generations. For one thing, Jax's old-world patio is like a secret garden with a fireplace, waterfall, shrubs, globe lanterns, and stream where you can catch your own trout and send it back to the kitchen to be cooked for your dinner. Another ritual is the elegant matchbook keepsake, manually embossed with your name and placed on your reserved table as you arrive.

Bill Kozlak Jr., who has owned the restaurant since 2000, has fond childhood memories of hanging out at the cozy, wood-paneled restaurant with his five siblings on Sundays when it was closed. "We'd come down here after church and have the place to ourselves," he said. "While Dad worked in the office, we'd run

around everywhere, talk on the loudspeaker, ride the elevators, and eat croutons in the kitchen."

Bill's great grandfather, Stanley Kozlak, first opened the place in 1910 to house his hardware, furniture, and funeral home businesses, as well as a local dance hall. When Prohibition ended in 1933, a guy named Jack Dusenka leased part of the building from Stanley and opened the bar and cafe, which could only seat about 50 at that time. He named it Jax instead of Jack's to make it more unique. In 1943, the Kozlak family took over the cafe and expanded it to include the entire main floor of the building. Today, it encompasses two full stories, including five banquet rooms adorned with wrought-iron chandeliers and French paintings lining the walls.

Jax Cafe is located within the Northeast Minneapolis Arts District, chock-full of live performance spaces and artist studios inside old factory buildings. Visit www.nemaa.org for site listings and events, including the annual Art-A-Whirl open studio tour in May.

Oldest Northside Theater

The Capri

2027 W Broadway Ave., Mpls. 55411

There's been a revival underway to bring back vitality to North Minneapolis. At the heart of that effort is the newly renovated and expanded Capri. The theater lights up West Broadway with top-notch concerts, plays, community events, and hands-on opportunities for youth to empower their creative spirits.

Originally known as the Logan Theater, then Paradise Theater, the Capri is the only survivor of what had once been 13 independent movie palaces on Minneapolis's Northside. In the early days, the theater was where children could spend Saturday afternoons watching cartoons on the big screen for a nickel and where adults relaxed in the evenings while being entertained by the likes of Humphrey Bogart and Audrey Hepburn.

In 1978, Ira "Smitty" Smith purchased the theater to provide positive influences for neighborhood youth, including serving as a music venue. On January 5, 1979, the Capri carved its rightful place in the rock 'n' roll pantheon when Prince played his first-ever solo show there. "He was cool, he was cocky, and he was sexy," wrote *Minneapolis Star* music critic Jon Bream. Those in attendance paid only $4.75 at the door.

Since 1984, PCYC, a service center focused on enriching the skills and prospects of North Minneapolis area youth and adults through the arts, has owned and occupied the theater. With the completion of a 20,000-square-foot expansion project in 2021, doubling its original size, the Capri now offers the community even more, including plays by Stages Theatre Company, music by the St. Paul Chamber Orchestra, and films presented in partnership with the MSP Film Society.

Part of the remodel includes a makeover of the original theater with new seats, lighting, and sound systems. Prince fans will be happy to know the stage floorboards are still the same ones on which the legend performed. Now, there's also a second theater space, scene shop, dance studio, and an ultramodern Best Buy Teen Tech Center. The expanded lobby highlights a gallery of Prince images by Greg Helgeson, who photographed the original concert. The building's updated exterior now includes a rain garden and plaza.

A half mile east of the Capri is Breaking Bread Cafe, where you can enjoy flavorful food celebrating the culinary legacy of Black Americans. It's operated by the nonprofit Appetite for Change.

$\overline{\hspace{3.5cm}}$1849

OLDEST NEIGHBORHOOD
MARCY-HOLMES
From U of M's Dinkytown to the riverfront

H ome of the iconic Stone Arch Bridge, Marcy-Holmes—
originally the town of St. Anthony Falls—is well
documented as Minneapolis's first neighborhood. But it's
also one of the hippest, dotted with eclectic architecture, river
trails, famous landmarks, and college-town pubs.

As a result of a controversial treaty negotiated by Lieutenant
Zebulon Pike in 1805, the Dakota homeland along both banks
of the Mississippi River became part of the Fort Snelling
Reservation. In 1838, Fort Snelling Commander Joseph
Plympton convinced the government to release the east side
for settlement, hoping to stake it for himself. In those days,
claiming land was a first-come, first-served affair. And this is
where a shrewd opportunist from Pennsylvania named Franklin
Steele enters Minnesota history.

Steele had recently started a job as storekeeper at Fort
Snelling. Upon hearing of Plympton's scheme, he embarked
on a "moonlight caper" up the river to the falls. There he built
a log shanty near present-day Second Avenue and Main Street
Southeast, beating Plympton to the punch. Steele's newly
acquired land gave him water rights to the falls, which used to
be one of the largest natural waterfalls in the US before the area
became heavily industrialized. Steele then built a mill and dam
with the help of Ard Godfrey.

In 1849, Steele platted St. Anthony, which was incorporated in 1855. By 1860, it was a favorite resort town for wealthy southerners who arrived by steamboats with their slaves to escape the heat. In 1872, the town voted to join Minneapolis, slowly flourishing on the other side of the river. Years later, the neighborhood was renamed in honor of politician William L. Marcy and poet Oliver Wendell Holmes.

IF YOU GO: A neighborhood audio tour, based on Penny Petersen's book *Hiding in Plain Sight: Minneapolis's First Neighborhood*, is available at www.minneapolishistorical.org.

Along Sixth Avenue SE, between University and Main, look for 24 miniature bronze sculptures of neighborhood landmarks, created by Aldo Moroni, including the Van Cleve Residence, Minneapolis's oldest continuously occupied home.

OLDEST STREET
MAIN STREET SOUTHEAST
East Bank/St. Anthony Main, Mpls. 55414

P aved with cobblestones and lined by gorgeous river views and historic buildings, Southeast Main Street is often mentioned as Minneapolis's prettiest and oldest street. One end intersects with Sixth Avenue with direct access to the Stone Arch Bridge and Father Hennepin Bluff Park while the other end continues into Northeast Minneapolis.

You'll stroll by a Segway tour agency, a cinema, a few charming patios and eateries—including the captivating Pracna on Main and the Aster Cafe—and Pillsbury A Mill, which was once the largest flour mill in the world, now transformed into artist lofts. The street is also where you can get up close to St. Anthony Falls at Xcel Energy Water Power Park, which commemorates the nation's first commercial hydroelectric generation station.

Before this area was developed in the mid-1850s, it was a vast wilderness. But as St. Anthony Falls became the center of lumber and flour industries, Main Street turned cosmopolitan. Shops, restaurants, hotels, and mills sprung up "like mushrooms." Back then, you could even take a 10-cent torchlight boat ride through the caves beneath the street.

During the 1920s, as the mill industries died out, Main Street was disinvested and forgotten. Enter architect Peter Nelson Hall, who, in 1968, became intrigued with the abandoned, red-brick, Queen Anne–style building at 117 Southeast Main Street. It was designed by Carl F. Struck in 1890 for Frank J. Pracna, a native of Bohemia, who operated a saloon on the site for many years.

In 1973, Hall and partner Tom Hanson revived Pracna as a restaurant and bar. It was an instant hit, although it has had its share of shutdowns since then. Soon after Pracna's success, the area was transformed into a festive marketplace. Unfortunately, that retail venture was short-lived. By the 1990s, the street became a "virtual ghost town." Today, the area continues to evolve as a culturally vital section of the city's birthplace.

Although Main Street is often mentioned as the city's oldest street, nearby Hennepin Avenue has roots that go back prior to Euro-American settlement when it was a corridor used by Indigenous people traveling from St. Anthony Falls to the shores of Bde Maka Ska.

Oldest Continuous Church
Our Lady of Lourdes Church
1 Lourdes Pl., Mpls. 55414

Poised above historic Main Street on the east side of the riverfront is a skinny, tall church with charming blue doors that looks like it belongs in Quebec. That's Our Lady of Lourdes, the oldest continuously operating church in Minneapolis.

The Greek Revival limestone church, built by the First Universalist Society, was dedicated in 1857. But membership soon began to wane after the parish's charismatic pastor, Reverend Bisbee, who was quite skeptical of well-known biblical miracles such as Noah's Ark, was found guilty of "heresy" by higher-ups. In 1877, it was sold to the Catholic, French-Canadian, St. Anthony of Padua Parish. They more than doubled the building size and added a bell tower, Gothic wooden steeple, and stained-glass windows. As a result, the church now resembles more of a French provincial style.

Insiders know Our Lady of Lourdes is the best spot in town to buy homemade French meat pies (*tourtieres*). Since the late 1800s, church volunteers have gathered to churn ground pork tenderloin, breadcrumbs, onions, and spices together to make the legendary pies for church fundraisers or to feed the homeless. Today, they're sold for $25 each from a little freezer in the entryway of the parish office next door. You can pick one up after Sunday Masses or by ringing the doorbell during weekday hours.

The parish was the first in the US to be named for the Marian apparitions that occurred in 1858 in the small town of Lourdes, France. The apparitions involved a humble, young girl by the name of Bernadette Soubirous, who is now canonized as a saint. She experienced 18 appearances of the Blessed Mary, Mother of Jesus, in a small cave near water, known as a grotto. Since the apparitions, the Grotto of Our Lady of Lourdes in France has become a famed sanctuary of grace, respect, unity, and healing to which thousands of people flock each year. You'll find a small reproduction of the grotto near the outside front entrance of Our Lady of Lourdes Church in Minneapolis.

Once you exit the church's front entrance, turn left and take a short stroll around the corner to Richard Chute Square at University Avenue and Bank Street, the site of the Ard Godfrey house (see next story).

1848–1849
OLDEST FRAME HOUSE
ARD GODFREY HOUSE
28 SE University Ave., Mpls. 55414

T he Ard Godfrey House, painted yellow and topped with two red brick chimneys, stands out like a ray of sunshine in Richard Chute Square, across from Lunds in St. Anthony Main. Step inside, and you're enveloped in warmth and simplicity while imagining a pioneer family sharing biscuits and tea in the parlor. As the oldest surviving frame house in the Twin Cities, it's surely an underrated gem.

In 1847, Ard Godfrey, a millwright from Maine, made his way to Minnesota, at the request of Franklin Steele, to supervise the building of the first commercial dam and lumber mill at St. Anthony Falls. His wife, Harriet, and their growing brood made the arduous journey to join him in 1849.

The one-and-a-half-story Greek Revival house, then located at the corner of Main Street and Second Avenue, was constructed in time for Harriet's arrival. Appointed as the town's first postmaster, Godfrey became a prominent member of the community while his wife's hospitality knew no bounds. Not surprisingly, their home became a popular gathering place.

In 1853, the Godfreys relocated to the Minnehaha Falls area. Various other families occupied the house until 1905, when it was sold to the Hennepin County Territorial Pioneers Association. Four years later, the association moved the house to its current spot in Chute Square and presented it to the

Minneapolis Park Board. In 1976, the home was impeccably restored by the Minneapolis Woman's Club as part of a US bicentennial project.

Today, members of the Woman's Club give tours of the home and its household artifacts. The summer tour season typically begins with Dandelion Day on the third Sunday in May. Visitors enjoy dandelion tea, learn recipes for dandelion salad and soup, and make dandelion crafts. This is in honor of Harriet Godfrey, who apparently was the first one to introduce Minnesota to the bright yellow plants after requesting a packet of seeds from her hometown. The rest was left to nature.

IF YOU GO: Free public tours on Saturdays and Sundays during summer months from 1–4 p.m. Visit www.minneapolisparks.org, and search "Ard Godfrey House" for updates.

The Godfreys offered to board nearly everyone who visited St. Anthony with visitors often sleeping on the floor of their yellow house. The parlor was where the first Masonic Lodge in Minnesota was formed with Godfrey as treasurer.

OLDEST ISLAND VENUE
NICOLLET ISLAND INN
95 Merriam St., Mpls. 55401

If you're looking for a venue with history and romance, it doesn't get more real than Nicollet Island Inn, a Victorian-style hotel and restaurant situated for more than a century on the Mississippi River's storied shores. To make it a full-on occasion, ask about their weekend Twilight River Cruise or take a local horse-drawn carriage tour.

The inn's allure begins with its thick limestone exterior accented by blue shutters, stained glass windows, flower boxes, gardens, awnings, twinkling lights, and vines. Once inside, you'll be captivated by the elegant details, from velvety drapes and tin ceilings to an antique glass elevator and a lounge bar with hand-carved maidenheads. In the basement, the old coal bin is now a patio dining area outside the banquet room.

The 48-acre island upon which the inn stands was used as a birthing place for Dakota women in ancient times. Today, it's a lovely parkland with trails, bridges, and an enclave of historic homes. In its lifetime, the island has gone through several radical transformations. At one time, it was filled with industry and commerce. The building that houses Nicollet Island Inn was first constructed in 1893 for Island Sash and Door Company, a wood-products factory. Today, it's one of two surviving industrial structures on the island. The other one is the Nicollet Island Pavilion, which is the shell of the former William Bros Boiler Works that's now a popular spot for weddings.

On a hot and windy day, less than a year after Island Sash and Door first opened, some boys smoking in a stable on the southwest side caused a fire that swept across the island. The majority of the island's buildings and 24 blocks of Northeast Minneapolis were turned to rubble. The Island Sash and Door Company was a lucky survivor and continued operations until 1899. Starting in 1913, it became a Salvation Army men's shelter for 60 years. In 1982, investors Ron Jacob and

Alan Fischlowitz purchased the building from the Minneapolis Park Board. They then hired architect David Shea, who transformed the building into the beautiful venue you see today.

On the path near the inn is a replica of a 2,000-year-old Dotaku Bell, a gift from Ibaraki, Japan. It's said if you ring the bell, a prayer is sent for world peace.

OLDEST TRAIN HUB

THE DEPOT

225 S 3rd Ave., Mpls. 55401

T he romantic notion of sitting in a plush train car while watching the countryside speed by through big windows lives on at the former Milwaukee Road Depot. Easily

identified by its clock tower modeled after the Giralda tower in Seville, Spain, the historic train hub is now a sprawling hospitality complex in the city's Mill District. Locals simply call it "the Depot."

Exploring its Great Hall and marble and brick corridors is truly a delight. Look for the 20-foot-high painting of a train crossing the Stone Arch Bridge, as well as "ghost statues" depicting true narratives of rail workers and passengers. Among them are Timothy, the shoeshine boy; Charley, the much-loved dining car waiter; Vivian, the suffrage advocate; and, of course, the reunited kissing couple.

Completed in 1899, the depot served as the end of the line for the Chicago, Milwaukee, St. Paul, and Pacific Railroad. It replaced an earlier version constructed in 1879. The only structure remaining from that original depot is the freight house at the corner of Third Avenue and Second Street, which now houses a Dunn Brothers coffeehouse. The freight house is listed in the National Register of Historic Places as Minneapolis's oldest surviving railway building.

The station's peak was in the 1920s when 29 trains departed daily. After the last train pulled out in 1971, it became a popular hangout for pigeons and homeless people while redevelopment plans fizzled. Finally, CSM Corporation purchased it in 1998 and began a massive renovation. The result was the Renaissance Minneapolis Hotel and the connecting Residence Inn while the train shed was transformed into a glass-encased ice rink, which has since been converted into a ballroom. The hotel also features the Milwaukee Road restaurant and a "hole in the wall" speakeasy hidden away on-site.

In May 1942, the Depot was the scene of mass excitement as the Hollywood Victory Caravan arrived carrying big stars raising funds for the war effort, from Groucho Marx and Joan Bennett to Bing Crosby and Bob Hope.

1822

OLDEST FLOUR MILL SITE
MILL RUINS PARK/MILL CITY MUSEUM
103 Portland Ave., Mpls. 55401

In 1822, the US Army opened Minnesota's first gristmill on the west bank of the Mississippi River near St. Anthony Falls. From this modest start, Minneapolis became the world's flour milling capital by 1880. There's no sign of that army mill today. But on that same site is Mill Ruins Park, a treasure trove of dilapidated mills that once served as the epicenter for Minneapolis's flour industry for 50 years. At the heart of it are the jagged-wall ruins of Washburn A Mill, where the process of turning wheat into premium flour was perfected.

Within the ruins of Washburn A Mill is Mill City Museum, a National Historic Landmark, where you can explore the city's milling history and learn where your Wheaties and Betty Crocker cake mixes come from. Don't miss Kevin Kling's humorous cinematic tour, "Minneapolis in 19 Minutes Flat," or the freight elevator ride up the structure known as the Flour Tower, during which machines come back to life and voices of former workers narrate the story of the mill.

Working in a flour mill had its share of occupational hazards. Workers lost fingers in machinery, fell into turbine pits, got buried alive inside grain silos, and fell victim to explosions. In 1874, Cadwallader Washburn, founder of the dynasty that's now General Mills, built the Washburn A Mill. In 1878, a spark ignited airborne flour dust, causing a thunderous explosion

that claimed 18 lives and destroyed much of the riverfront area. Two years later, the mill was rebuilt and was soon leading the world in flour, producing enough to make 12 million loaves of bread in a day.

The mill closed in 1965, remaining vacant for more than two decades. A devastating fire gutted the abandoned mill in 1991 but presented an opportunity. The Minnesota Historical Society decided to preserve the ruins and utilize as much of the original building as possible while creating a place for the public to learn about the city's rich history.

IF YOU GO: The museum is open Thursday through Sunday. Admission ranges $8–$12.

After exploring the ruins and museum, head up to the nearby Guthrie Theater's fourth floor Endless Bridge, which juts out about 180 feet from the building, offering panoramic river views. The ninth floor, featuring floor-to-ceiling, yellowish-tinted windows, provides a cool view too. Free and open to the public.

OLDEST BRIDGE RELICS
FIRST BRIDGE PARK
1 W River Pkwy., Mpls. 55401

Just past Mill Ruins Park, at the base of the Hennepin Avenue Bridge, is First Bridge Park, the site of the first bridge to span the Mississippi River—anywhere. Underneath the current bridge are old cables and anchors from the bridge's predecessors, discovered during archeological excavations in the 1980s.

Until the 1850s, the rocky ledge above St. Anthony Falls was the only place to cross the mighty river in the area. This was easy enough if there was a thick layer of ice, but it got tricky with the high, rushing waters in spring and summer. To make the trek easier in the short term, businessmen Franklin Steele and John Stevens established a rope ferry in 1847.

A few years later, Steele pulled together a group of investors to construct

a 620-foot-long wooden suspension bridge that stretched from the West Bank to Nicollet Island. Despite the cold, locals celebrated the momentous occasion on January 23, 1855, with a gala and mile-long parade. The bridge was considered one of the most elegantly engineered structures in the country, featuring tall wooden towers and wire suspension cables.

Crossing the bridge required tolls to be paid. A lone pedestrian paid three cents one way. But if the travelers had any horses or mules with them, they'd have to pay 15 cents for each. In contrast, the cost if they were accompanied by a pig or sheep was only two cents. That first bridge quickly deteriorated, though, and was replaced by a succession of three other bridges, including the current bridge constructed in 1990. Interpretive markers and etchings at the park highlight the site's history.

IF YOU GO: First Bridge Park is situated along the St. Anthony Falls Heritage Trail, a 1.8-mile loop along the Minneapolis riverfront.

Look for little bronze toads and turtles embedded along the park's curvy seat wall and a large piece of native limestone that stands as a tribute to Wanaǵi Wita (Spirit Island), a former native site lost to quarrying.

Oldest Northloop Bar
Monte Carlo
219 N 3rd Ave., Mpls. 55401

Also known as the Minneapolis Warehouse District, the Northloop is one of the state's trendiest neighborhoods with no shortage of artsy places to eat, drink, shop, and live. But at the same time, its history as a wholesaling and manufacturing epicenter filled with factories built from the 1880s to the early 1930s along the railroad tracks is uniquely preserved.

Milky Way candy bars, Creamette pasta, and the world's first pop-up toaster were among the products born in the North Loop. As you walk around, notice the brick pavers, salvaged train lines and tracks, original bridges, and vintage warehouse buildings. The historic neighborhood has more than 60 buildings that are over a century old. While still bearing faded original company logos, many of the old warehouses have been repurposed into residential lofts, visual art centers, and even costume shops and rehearsal spaces for the Minnesota Opera.

Not all the original businesses have faded, though. The Monte Carlo Bar and Grill, for example, has stood the test of time. Its vintage atmosphere features floral wallpaper, photos of famous patrons, white tablecloths, and a snazzy copper bar with about a thousand liquor bottles stacked up against a mirrored wall. Originally opened as one of Gluek's bars in 1902 (look for the "G" still imprinted on the original tin ceiling), the venue has been known as Monte Carlo since 1906.

The restaurant component was added when John Rimarcik purchased it in 1982 from longtime owner Steve Critelli. Prior to that, it was mostly a saloon frequented by men. Under Rimarcik's leadership, it has become a destination for all. In the summer, its large patio is a beautiful oasis for enjoying ice-cold martinis, steaks, chops, seafood, and their famous Beijing-style chicken wings.

The Northloop is named for a segment of an old streetcar system that once looped around the Warehouse District on the northern edge of downtown.

OLDEST SKYSCRAPER
LUMBER EXCHANGE BUILDING
10 S 5th St., Mpls. 55402

U ntil lumber supplies were depleted in the early 20th century, all the stars aligned for Minneapolis to become a sawmill empire. There was the magnificent growth of white pine to the north, the Mississippi River for transporting cut logs, and the hydropower of St. Anthony Falls to convert those logs into merchantable boards.

The place where all the trading deals took place between wealthy timber barons in double-breasted frock coats was the

Lumber Exchange Building. The rugged, red granite heap with impish faces and beasts carved into its exterior was designed by Franklin B. Long and Frederick Kees, who also designed Minneapolis City Hall and the nearby Masonic Temple.

Back in the day, a skyscraper was a

term used to refer to buildings between 10 and 20 stories. The Lumber Exchange Building was Minneapolis's first. It's also the oldest structure outside of New York City with at least 12 floors and is one of the first fireproof skyscrapers in the country.

Look way up at the top two stories, and notice the subtle change in brick color. That's because it was originally built as a narrow, 10-floor structure. Five years later, Long and Kees more than doubled the building's floor area with a two-story addition to the top and a 12-story extension along Hennepin Avenue. The interior features marble floors, brick walls, chandeliers, arch entries, and brass elevators accented by stained glass ceilings and pictures of grain silos.

Today, the building houses an eclectic mix of businesses. On the third floor is the Lumber Exchange Event Center's dazzling, nine-story atrium. On the ground floor is the main entrance to the Pourhouse, a Prohibition-themed bar. And in the winding cave-like basement, which once served as a Turkish bathhouse for lumber executives, you can dance the night away on weekends in the Exchange and Alibi Lounge. Its name is a reference to a barber shop once housed in the building and used by notorious gangster Kid Cann as an alibi to avoid murder charges when accused of killing *Minneapolis Star* newspaper editor Walter Liggett in 1935.

The building's main entrance on Hennepin Avenue features a brass revolving door that once connected Grand Central Station in New York to the adjacent Commodore Hotel for 100 years.

1902/1934
OLDEST DOWNTOWN BAR
GLUEK'S
16 N 6th St., Mpls. 55403

Across from Butler Square and along First Avenue, you'll see a long mural of gondolas gliding through the canals of Venice. The mural was created a couple of decades ago by Bavarian artist Hermann Krumpholz. But the real story

is the old-world establishment housed inside the building it's painted on—Gluek's, beautifully restored after suffering a major fire in 1989.

Gluek's is a favorite designation for grabbing a beer and German fare before or after an event at nearby Target Field or Target Center. Its interior is reminiscent of an old European beer hall with dark paneling, high ceilings, stained glass windows, and mounted buffalo, deer, and moose heads curiously lit up by multicolored Christmas lights.

The terra-cotta structure was built in 1902 by Gluek Brewing Company as an outlet bar to sell their beers until it closed

during Prohibition. The current fourth-generation owner Dave Holcomb's great grandfather purchased the bar from Gluek's in 1934. He operated it as Fransen's Bar and Restaurant until the name was changed back to Gluek's in 1979.

Although there's no longer any business connection between the downtown establishment and Gluek's beer brand, they have similar roots tracing back to 1857. That's when German immigrant Gottlieb Gluek established his brewery in Northeast Minneapolis while using caves on the north end of Nicollet Island to age his lagers. The brewery and mansion were demolished in 1966 after Gluek sold out to a competitor. That site is now home to Gluek Park. Coldspring Brewery later acquired the brand but retired it in 2010. The beer brand was revived in 2017 and is now available again throughout the state.

Fun fact: The buffalo head in the back room of Gluek's was once stolen by fraternity members from a local college. Fortunately, it was anonymously returned—left propped against the front door on the day the place reopened following the 1989 fire.

Oldest Improv Company
Brave New Workshop
824 Hennepin Ave., Mpls. 55403

For generations, Minnesotans have been stereotyped as polite and mild-mannered. But that surely hasn't stopped locals from staking out seats at Brave New Workshop, where politicians and celebrities are skewered and topics entirely inappropriate for "Minnesota Nice" take center stage. Not only is it a local comedic powerhouse, but it's also the longest-running live-sketch comedy improv company in the nation.

It all started with a witty, bow-tied fella named Dudley Riggs, who grew up in a traveling circus and made everybody around him feel like they belonged. Born in Little Rock, Arkansas, to a pair of trapeze artists, he started his own aerial act. But after a near-fatal fall, he focused on theater instead, forming the Instant Theater Company with a cast of performers from his circus and vaudeville circles.

After touring around the country, Riggs settled in Minneapolis in 1958 and opened the city's first espresso coffeehouse on East Hennepin. It became a place where funny people hung out and performed impromptu, audience-driven sketches. In 1965, Riggs found a new venue, a former auto repair shop in the Uptown area. It was under that roof where Brave New Workshop (BNW), named in honor of Aldous Huxley's novel *Brave New World*, grew into a legend for four decades.

Now housed in the former Hennepin Stages Theatre in downtown, BNW has been a breeding ground for many successful careers, including Susan Vass, Al Franken, and Louie Anderson. In 1997, Riggs sold the theater to John Sweeney and Jenni Lilledahl, who rolled out a red carpet for Riggs before every opening show thereafter. In 2014, Sweeney and Lilledahl purchased an additional building for offering workshops related to comedy, innovation, and leadership.

Dudley Riggs died at age 88 on September 22, 2020, in the throes of the global pandemic that shut his beloved theater down for two years. As they say, he always was a master of good timing. In December 2021, Hennepin Theatre Trust purchased the venue, pledging to bring back live productions and continue Dudley Riggs's legacy.

"It's not the passing laugh we're looking for. It's a laugh that people can have while at the theater but then argue about on the way home."—Dudley Riggs, My North, *Episode 49*

————————————————————1914

OLDEST BASILICA IN AMERICA
BASILICA OF ST. MARY
1600 Hennepin Ave., Mpls. 55403

Y ou don't have to be affiliated with a specific religion to marvel over the Basilica of St. Mary, that copper-domed Beaux-Arts treasure dominating an entire block near the heart of downtown. More than a house of worship, it's a center for the arts, a refuge for those in need, and a place for drop-in visitors to sit quietly for a moment.

Worldwide, there are four major basilicas and more than 1,800 minor basilicas. Of the 89 minor basilicas in the US, St. Mary's was the first. The Basilica of St. Mary, whose members hail from 434 different zip codes, took root inside a little "shed church" at Third Street and Third Avenue North. Built in 1868, it was known as the Church of the Immaculate Conception. A larger church was built for the parish at the same site in 1871.

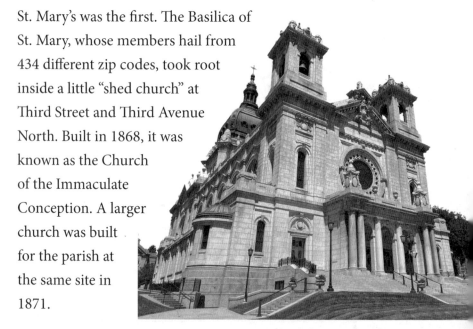

Then, on August 1, 1905, Archbishop John Ireland announced his grand vision to build the parish a pro-cathedral (a term given prior to the designation of cathedral) simultaneously with the extravagant St. Paul Cathedral. The first Mass in Minneapolis's grand structure was held in 1914. Pope Pius XI elevated the church to a minor basilica honoring St. Mary in 1926.

On the west side of the Basilica is the serene Mary Garden, where visitors can pause and pray. Out front to the right, along Hennepin Avenue, is a life-size sculpture of Jesus shrouded in a blanket on a park bench, designed to inspire compassion for the homeless. To the left is the towering bronze statue of Father Louis Hennepin, who was the first European to discover St. Anthony Falls in 1680, naming it after St. Anthony of Padua. (Long before that, however, the Falls were named *Owámniyomni*, meaning "turbulent waters," by the Dakota people who frequently visited the site for sacred ceremonies.)

Inside highlights include stained glass windows representing Christian narratives, many depictions of saints and of Mary, and marble statues portraying the apostles surrounding the sanctuary. On the lower level is the Pope John XXIII Gallery displaying artwork spanning five centuries. The Basilica is open to the public Monday through Friday 9 a.m. to 5 p.m.

"Basilica" is an esteemed title bestowed by the Vatican that permits certain distinctions, including special ceremonial precedence over other Catholic churches.

Oldest Nicollet Mall Art

Sculpture Clock

11th St. and Nicollet, Mpls. 55403

Stretching from Loring Park to the Mississippi River, Nicollet Avenue has long been the heartbeat of downtown. In 1967, it became the nation's first transit mall after landscape architect Lawrence Halprin transformed eight blocks of the corridor into the tree-lined, no-automobiles-allowed retail experience we know today.

Completely renovated in 2017 after more than two years of construction, the mall is a charming place to stroll and shop amid fountains, planters, sparkly lights, movable seating, and public art, including decorative manhole covers by Kate Burke and bronze ghost shadows set into the pavement by Seitu Jones and Ta-coumba Aiken. The only remaining art remnant of Halprin's 1960s design is the Sculpture Clock, dedicated on October 7, 1968.

The 21-foot-high clock, now situated next to Orchestra Hall and Peavey Plaza (a lovely spot accentuated by stepped terraces and cascading water features), highlights a perpetually whirling brass mobile made up of more than 500 moving parts enclosed inside an unbreakable glass case. Kristin Cheronis, local professional preservationist, provided this description of the mechanics of the Sculpture Clock: "When in motion,

the various whirligig-like elements installed along the shafts interact with each other playfully; twirling and swinging, swaying, jumping and jiggling."

Handcrafted by Jack Nelson, artist and professor at Syracuse University, the rare kinetic timepiece ran continuously from 1968 until 2002. That's when the motors died out, and the city declined to order new ones due to cost. By the time it was de-installed for the 2017 mall renovation, its metal elements had become corroded and tarnished.

Cheronis, whose team was hired to assess and restore the clock, declared the clock to be in the worst condition of all 64 artworks owned by the city at the time. After its artistic and historic significance was finally acknowledged and grant applications were submitted, the Arts and Cultural Heritage Fund, through the Minnesota Historical Society, awarded the necessary funds to begin the yearlong restoration process.

For photos and stories about other public art on Nicollet Mall, check out nicolletmallart.org.

A block south of the clock, across from Westminster Presbyterian Church, is an entrance to Loring Greenway, a treasured urban pathway connecting Nicollet Mall to Loring Park.

Oldest "Best Bar"
Palmer's Bar
500 Cedar Ave., Mpls. 55454

"**S**orry, we're open," the sign says. With an Islamic Mosque connected to it on one end and that image of a beer-holding, mustachioed man sporting a bowler hat and bow tie leaning against it on the other, Palmer's Bar is a place you rarely leave without a story to tell.

Located in the Cedar-Riverside neighborhood, often dubbed "Little Somalia" or "Little United Nations" for its diverse population, Palmer's is the quintessential hole-in-the-wall with a mixed bag of regulars and a spirit all its own. Known as Palmer's since 1950, it first opened as a workingman's beer hall in 1906. The interior has remained mostly unchanged over the decades—same red-and-white tiled floor and same tiny, trapezoid-shaped, back-corner stage.

Palmer's is one of the oldest bars in Minneapolis, but it's also the oldest of a handful of Minneapolis bars named to *Esquire's* annual "Best Bars in America" list over the years. This came about in 2014 after David Wondrich, a world-renowned authority on the history of the cocktail, paid a visit. He said he found his way there after asking the scruffiest local he could find at the public library about his favorite hangout.

Palmer's surely isn't suited for everyone's tastes. But whatever your gender, race, or creed, you're invited to belly up to the bar for a good stiff drink, join a pickup Scrabble game, or gather around the patio campfire for deep conversation. That is, unless you start acting like a jerk. If you do, there's a good chance you'll get booted out and have your name added to the Wall of Shame behind the bar, a longtime tradition.

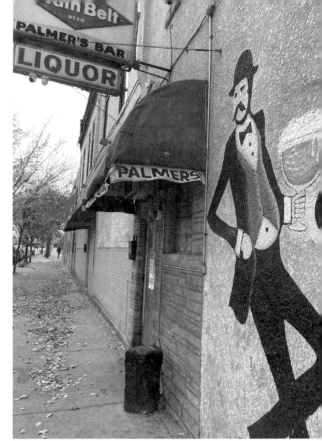

There have been at least a dozen owners throughout the decades. Tony Zaccardi bought the bar from Lisa Hammer in 2018. Lisa had co-owned it for 14 years with her husband, Keith Berg, until he unexpectedly died at age 56 in 2015. Zaccardi, a bass player for various bands—including Eleganza and Romantica—was propelled into the national spotlight in 2020 after he spray-painted "Black Owned Business" on his bar to deflect potential looters following George Floyd's death.

"Palmer's has been described as: a church for down and outers and those who romanticize them, a rare place where high and low rub elbows—bums and poets, thieves and slumming celebrities" (Palmer's website).

1975

OLDEST AMERICAN INDIAN CENTER

MINNEAPOLIS AMERICAN INDIAN CENTER

1530 E Franklin Ave., Mpls. 55404

The Franklin Avenue East Cultural District in South Minneapolis is home to one of the country's largest concentrations of urban Indigenous people. The area has gone through rough times, but today we see a renaissance with an eight-block section of East Franklin Avenue designated as an American Indian Cultural Corridor, spotlighting Native American art, food, and culture.

A central focus of the corridor involves the Minneapolis American Indian Center (MAIC). Opened in 1975, the MAIC is one of the oldest urban American Indian Centers in the nation. Since then, it has evolved as a centerpiece of community resources and events, including family fun nights, language arts and nutrition workshops, and drum and dance performances.

In addition to gathering spaces and gyms, the MAIC houses the Woodland Crafts Gift Shop, Two Rivers Art Gallery, and Gatherings Cafe, focused on contemporary Indigenous flavors. In Summer 2022, the center began a major renovation scheduled to be completed by Summer 2025. The redesign will expand the center with a glass-wall front along Franklin to showcase the gift shop, gallery, and restaurant. MAIC programs will continue at remote sites throughout the renovations.

One block from the MAIC, along the same corridor, you'll see a bright yellow and orange building. Housed inside is Pow Wow Grounds, a great place to enjoy a good cup of coffee and a blueberry wild rice muffin. Under the same roof is the All My Relations Art Gallery, devoted to elevating the visibility of contemporary Native artists. Look for the mural by Natchez Beaulieu painted on the building's exterior, featuring a woman with braids cascading into a waterfall. The red handprint muzzling the woman's mouth symbolizes solidarity for missing and murdered Indigenous women. The cityscape and teepee reflected in her sunglasses represent the grand vision for this culturally rich pocket of the Twin Cities.

For a true background of the American Indian Cultural Corridor, start with the "Unholy Tour." Visit www.oyatehotanin.org for more information.

The Minneapolis American Indian Center is the heart of East Franklin Avenue, which was the birthplace of the far-reaching grassroots American Indian Movement that began taking form in 1968 to combat discrimination against Native Americans.

The eastern wall of the MAIC features a 3,300-square-foot, three-panel mural by artists Gregg Deal and Votan Henriquez. Along the building's East Franklin Avenue entrance, a large-scale geometric wood collage by artist George Morrison overlooks an amphitheater. Photo was taken prior to renovations.

OLDEST LIBRARY
FRANKLIN LIBRARY
1314 E Franklin Ave., Mpls. 55404

C omfy chairs huddle around historic fireplaces while soft light filters through frosted glass ceiling panels. Posted fliers announce a panel discussion on the meaning of home and exile. Hennepin County's Franklin Library is a beautiful temple of information. But with roots dating back to 1890, it's also been the heart of the immigrant community through wars, epidemics, homelessness, injustice, and civil unrest.

While North Branch on Emerson is the city's oldest surviving library building, Franklin Library, which was first organized in a couple of rented rooms two blocks away, is the oldest one still serving as a library. Franklin's current building, constructed in 1914, was the first of four Minneapolis Public Library buildings financed by Scottish steel tycoon Andrew Carnegie. During his lifetime, Carnegie donated $45 million to construct more than 1,600 libraries across America; 66 of them (of which 48 are still standing) were built here in Minnesota.

Added to the National Register of Historic Places in 2000 and renovated in 2004 and 2020, Franklin Library continues to prove its relevance by offering citizenship classes and community workshops on housing, day care, health, employment, legal issues, and alcoholism.

On the east end is an entire section of Native American literature, featuring memoirs, essays, poetry, and historical

texts by Native authors, available to borrow through the library system's holds-pickup feature. Above the nearby fireplace is a mosaic titled *Red Lake* by Robert DesJarlait, dedicated to victims of the 2005 school shootings on the Red Lake Reservation. A mosaic above the fireplace on the west end, titled *World Language* by Marilyn Lindstrom, includes ancient symbols for the globe's seven continents.

Franklin Library was one of 13 branch libraries established under the leadership of Gratia Countryman, the nation's first female head librarian, often referred to as the "First Lady of Minneapolis."

Oldest Washburn-Fair Oaks Mansion

Eugene Merrill Mansion

2116 S 2nd Ave., Mpls. 55404

The Washburn-Fair Oaks Mansion District is a place of grand architecture and history. Centered around Washburn-Fair Oaks Park, across from the Minneapolis Institute of Arts, it was once home to the biggest mansions in Minneapolis, occupied by prestigious families such as the Pillsburys, the Turnblads, and, of course, the Washburns.

Most of the area's first-generation mansions fell to the wrecking ball, but several are still standing. The oldest of those is the 1884 rustic red sandstone estate with the polygonal tower at

2116 Second Avenue South. Its first occupant was banker and lawyer Eugene Merrill, his wife Addie, and their four children. It was later converted into a rest home for the elderly and then an art gallery. Today, it houses a law firm.

That's not the only original mansion near the park to be repurposed. The George H. Christian Mansion at 2303 Third Avenue South is now home to the Hennepin History Museum, a wonderful resource devoted to social history. The mansion at 100 East Twenty-Second Street, built for Charles Pillsbury Jr., houses a school for the blind. And the Gale Mansion at 2115 Stevens Avenue is a special events venue.

The park itself is named for a castle-like edifice that once stood there on a 10-acre lot, encompassing 40 rooms, a carriage house, lake, and pond. It was built in 1884 for William D. Washburn, brother of Cadwallader Washburn, founder of the Washburn Crosby Mill, which later became General Mills. In 1915, after both Washburns had died, the Park Board took control of the property until it was demolished in 1924, despite considerable protest. While at the park, look for the information sign about the long-gone mansion, including photos, at the corner of Stevens Avenue and Twenty-Second Street.

Combine your house gawking with a visit to the Minneapolis Institute of Arts (free general admission), followed by a meal on Eat Street, a stretch of Nicollet Avenue nearby that features some of Minneapolis's most beloved restaurants distinguished by diversity and history.

OLDEST FOOD CO-OP
SEWARD COMMUNITY CO-OP
2823 E Franklin Ave., Mpls. 55406

I n 1969, an assortment of flower-child hippies converged in a commune in the nearly abandoned town of Georgeville, 90 minutes northwest of Minneapolis. This industrious bunch, "who were as keen on broccoli as pot and LSD" (*Co-op News*), began growing their own food while plotting a more

equitable alternative to corporate capitalism. The eventual result was revolutionary.

Inspired by San Francisco's network of collectively owned, no-frills, natural food shops, the group's founders soon launched their own

Seward Co-op, est. 1972. Courtesy Seward Co-op

enterprise from a back porch in Minneapolis's West Bank. It was a volunteer-led operation, known as the People's Pantry, where participants could scoop sesame seeds, whole wheat flour, and brown rice from bulk bins at low prices.

People's Pantry merged with a small grocery store and incorporated as North Country Co-op. Its massive popularity ignited a surge of local co-ops so big that by the mid-1970s, Minnesota had more co-ops than anywhere in the country.

Established in 1972, Seward Co-op was among the earliest. Today, Seward encompasses more than 21,000 invested households and two locations (including the "Friendship Store" on Thirty-Eighth Street) and lays claim to being the oldest collectively managed business in the Twin Cities.

The Twin Cities co-op movement wasn't all peace and love, though. A bitter battle over food policies and political agendas began brewing in the shadows. Veteran radicals entered the scene, rejecting the pioneer co-op movement as "white bourgeois elitism." The conflict erupted in Spring 1975 when a belligerent group (called the Co-op Organization), who announced they represented the working class, broke into the main co-op distribution site armed with steel bars and firebombs. Although the friction had a debilitating effect, the attempt to seize the co-ops by force failed. Today, the Twin Cities co-op scene is still one of the country's most vibrant.

To learn more about the local food co-op culture that nearly collapsed with a violent struggle, check out the documentary The Co-op Wars (2021), *directed by Deacon Warner and produced by Erik Esse.*

OLDEST SCI-FI BOOKSTORE

UNCLE HUGO'S

2716 E 31st St., Mpls. 55406

I n the early hours of Saturday, May 30, 2020, Don Blyly, owner of Uncle Hugo's Science Fiction Bookstore, the oldest of its genre in America, along with its companion

Uncle Hugo's new home on 31st Street

shop, Uncle Edgar's Mystery Bookstore, received a call from his store's security company. The motion detector was showing somebody in the building. He hopped in his car and rushed right over.

By the time Blyly arrived at his beloved, literary treasure on Chicago Avenue, flames were leaping out the front windows. In fact, every building on both sides of the street was blazing as part of widespread civil unrest in the days following the police killing of George Floyd. Within just a few hours, Blyly's business, which he'd poured himself into for 46 years, had been reduced to a pile of rubble.

With a knack for overcoming adversity, though, Blyly is bouncing back. After two long years of trials and tribulations, his twin bookstores, fondly known as "the Uncles," reopened in a shared space in August 2022, about two miles east of the previous location. Thousands of donated books have been pouring in from loyal customers overjoyed about the reopening. But nobody is happier than Blyly's dog, Ecko, who now has his job back as everybody's favorite store greeter.

Blyly first opened Uncle Hugo's in 1974 when he was a law student at the University of Minnesota. Bored by constitutional law, he thought operating a bookstore would be a fun distraction. The store is named after Hugo Gernsback, who started the first

Courtesy Mina Blyly-Strauss

science fiction magazine. Six years later, he opened Uncle Edgar's, named for Edgar Allan Poe, in a nearby location. Blyly first moved the two stores into a connected space at the previous Chicago Avenue location in 1984.

The bookstore's new 5,000-square-foot building (former home of Glass Endeavors) was likely to have been built between 1925 and 1927. It contains an original walk-in safe from when it housed a post office as well as a large 1940 mural of Minnehaha Falls permanently painted onto an interior wall.

OLDEST HIKING TRAIL
WINCHELL TRAIL
4357 W River Pkwy., Mpls. 55406

Nature meets history on the Winchell Trail, a roughly five-mile, out-and-back, full-immersion escape in the heart of the city. Winding along the Mississippi River bluffs, from Forty-Fourth Street to Franklin Avenue, it follows what was most likely an original path created by the Dakota people who lived near the river's shores centuries ago. The trail marker indicates that it was established in 1883 as the Minneapolis Park System's first rustic hiking trail.

The trail was named for Newton Horace Winchell, a leading geologist of the late 19th century and professor at the University of Minnesota. Among Winchell's many outstanding contributions were his published works about measurements and time frames related to the glacial age. The estimates he made in 1878, using historical maps and scientific reasoning, were remarkably close to modern estimates based on sophisticated radiometric dating techniques.

Unpaved trails break away from the main trail and cut deep into the woods, permitting additional exploration of the Mississippi Gorge. One section takes you down to the river. Another leg crosses an oak savanna restoration, one of the state's rarest native plant communities. The trail features several stone walls and staircases marked with the Works

Progress Administration (WPA) stamp, a federal government program that created jobs to help lift the country out of the Great Depression while building many park features in the 1930s and 1940s.

IF YOU GO: A good place to hop on the trail is from the small parking lot across the street from the Becketwood Retirement home. On the south side of the parking lot, look for a path that leads down to an information sign about the trail's history. The Minneapolis Parks Foundation offers printable guides for their most popular trails, including Winchell Trail. Go to www.mplsparksfoundation.org, type "self-guided tours"' in the search bar, and click on the Walk and Talk series.

Near the north end of Winchell Trail, at the intersection of Franklin Avenue and West River Parkway, sits a taconite boulder. It's from the Mesabi Iron Range commemorating the scientific contributions of the trail's namesake: Newton Horace Winchell, Minnesota's first state geologist.

OLDEST PRESERVATION
JOHN H. STEVENS HOUSE
4901 S Minnehaha Ave., Mpls. 55417

May 28, 1896, was a rootin' tootin' day for Minneapolis schoolchildren. That was the day the *Minneapolis Journal* rallied an estimated 10,000 squirrely, mostly unchaperoned kids to skip class and hop on a trolley for free to help move an old, rotting, timber house six miles across town in a campaign to keep it from being demolished.

Organized into relay teams, the students grabbed onto long ropes attached to horses and followed their orders: Forward, march! Hoisted on wheels, the house creaked and groaned as it was pulled to Minnehaha Falls Regional Park, where the kids were rewarded with peanuts, popcorn, and lemonade.

1896, MNHS Collections

This wasn't just any old house. Constructed in 1850 near the present-day Minneapolis Post Office, it was the first authorized house built west of the Mississippi River in the area that would become Minneapolis. US Army Colonel John H. Stevens and his wife, Frances Helen Miller, received permission

to occupy the site, a part of Fort Snelling at the time, in exchange for providing ferry service at St. Anthony Falls. This home is where the city of Minneapolis was named and Hennepin County was organized.

Photo taken in May 2022, prior to the recent fires.

It's where the judicial system was established, first elections were held, streets were named, and the first school district was formed.

The Junior League of Minneapolis, which restored the home in the 1980s, called the historic relocation the earliest example of historic preservation in Minneapolis. In 1983, the home was moved deeper within the park. To commemorate the 1896 move, schoolchildren were once again recruited to help. This time, though, the ropes were attached to a truck.

Near the Stevens House are the 1875 "Princess Depot," a tiny restored railroad depot that resembles a gingerbread house, and the yellow 1907 Longfellow House, a replica of Henry W. Longfellow's home in Cambridge, MA.

UPDATE: *Tragically, the John H. Stevens House was significantly damaged in a series of fires in late summer/early fall of 2022. Investigation and damage assessments were still underway as this book went into production. Any reopening status will be posted at www.minneapolisparks.org.*

OLDEST CEMETERY
PIONEERS AND SOLDIERS MEMORIAL CEMETERY
2945 S Cedar Ave., Mpls. 55407

While strolling amid the slanted, chipped, and faded headstones of Pioneers and Soldiers Memorial Cemetery—the oldest in Minneapolis—one can only imagine the poignant life stories of those who lived and breathed the pioneering chapters of Minneapolis history.

Originally called Layman's Cemetery after its founders, Martin and Elizabeth Layman, this unpretentious place is one of the few cemeteries inducted into the National Register of Historic Places. That honor is attributed, in large part, to its social history. Since the plots were less expensive than those at competing cemeteries, many of those buried here were from the working classes of pioneers and immigrants who slaved over spinning wheels and washtubs, harvested corn fields, laid down railroad tracks, and worked in the mills.

Although the cemetery was deemed full in 1919, visitors may wonder why it feels so empty. There were about 22,000 burials, but there are only about 2,100 marked graves. Many markers have been destroyed by vandals or Minnesota winters. In many cases, a marker was never purchased because of extreme poverty.

More than half of the people buried in the cemetery were children due to communicable diseases and the high infant mortality rate. One of the cemetery's saddest stories, collected and published in *Hennepin History* magazine by Friends of the

Cemetery member Susan Weir, include a widowed mother of eight (and another eight dead in childhood) who took her own life on her husband's grave in 1909. Another is of the 25 infants who died while at Cody Hospital, a so-called "baby farm," between 1908 and 1909.

Because the founders had strong ties to the abolitionist movement, it was one of the few unsegregated cemeteries of its time. It holds several hundred of the city's early African American residents, including Civil War veteran Oscar Vaughn, Minneapolis's first black firefighter Captain John W. Cheatham, and Underground Railroad Station Master William C. Goodridge. True to its name, the cemetery also holds the remains of about 200 military veterans who fought in the many American conflicts, from the War of 1812 to the Korean War.

Next to the cemetery's historic limestone caretaker's cottage is a memorial dedicated to the city's courageous, but often forgotten, Pioneer Mothers. Look for the words of Abraham Lincoln: "All that I am, or hope to be, I owe to my angel mother."

OLDEST NORDIC CENTER
INGEBRETSEN'S NORDIC MARKETPLACE
1601 E Lake St., Mpls. 55407

T ough and resilient, Lake Street is a six-mile commercial corridor through the heart of South Minneapolis where countless dreams have been made and broken.

For more than a century, the street has been a destination

for immigrants, from Norwegians, Germans, and Swedes to Somalis, Ethiopians, and Latinos. Many poured their life savings into owning little shops and eateries while doing their best to survive suburban flight, disinvestment, the pandemic, and violent destruction in 2020. At the heart of the community is Ingebretsen's Nordic Marketplace, family-operated since 1921.

This whimsically painted deli and gift shop is more than a place where you can get all the lutefisk, lingonberry jam, and needlework your heart desires. It's a connection to another place and time. It's especially magical in the weeks leading up to Christmas with lines of customers stretched down the block and shelves overflowing with reindeer crafts, cozy sweaters, and homemade tree ornaments.

Ingebretsen's is the Twin Cities' oldest retail business dedicated to Scandinavian heritage and one of the longest-surviving immigrant businesses on East Lake Street. It was started by Karl "Charlie" Ingebretsen as a butcher shop named Model Market, known for Swedish meatballs and potato sausages. In the 1960s, Karl's son, "Bud," and expert meat cutter Warren Dahl joined the business. Shortly after, they renamed it Ingebretsen's and expanded to include a gift shop, managed by Bud's daughter, Julie Ingebretsen, for 50 years.

Julie has played a pivotal role in connecting customers to the traditions of their ancestors by adding a thriving mail-order service, a children's section, and a separate room for year-round classes in Nordic crafts and culture. She's also been instrumental in the inspiring, ongoing recovery of Lake Street. Fourth-generation Ingebretsens, along with descendants of Warren Dahl, are now helping to carry the legacy forward.

About a mile from Ingebretsen's is the Norway House, which houses a Nordic-themed art gallery, a new genealogy center, and a second Ingebretsen's business called Also Ingebretsen's.

OLDEST BOWLING ALLEY

BRYANT LAKE BOWL

810 W Lake St., Mpls. 55408

Bowling might be the oldest game in history. A century ago, British anthropologist Sir Flinders Petrie discovered a primitive bowling set tucked inside a 5,000-year-old Egyptian tomb. The history of bowling in the Twin Cities doesn't hold a candle to that, but there are a few places where folks have been knocking down pins for generations.

Minneapolis's oldest bowling alley is Bryant Lake Bowl, an Uptown landmark with eight vintage lanes bordered by red, yellow, and black checkered tile floors. Locally nicknamed the BLB, it opened in 1936 in a former garage that had serviced Model T Fords. Longtime regulars can recite the line "You don't have to go home, but you can't stay here," spoken into the microphone at closing time for many years by Roger Engmark, who started working there in the 1970s.

In 1959, the bowling alley was bought by Minnesota Bowling Hall of Famer Bill Drouches, who installed the automatic pinsetters still in use today. In 1993, ownership was passed on to mega restaurateur Kim Bartmann, who transformed the shoe counter into a kitchen, classied up the drink and food menu, and—while retaining the bowling lanes—converted the game room into a 90-seat cabaret theater with old red seats from the Stillwater Junior High auditorium. The theater hosts an assortment of events from plays and concerts to movie screenings and discussions on the

environment. In 2018, Bartmann sold the venue to longtime employee Erica Gilbert.

If you haven't already seen it, search online for the genius 90-second drone video featuring Bryant Bowl, entitled "Right Up Our Alley" that went viral in 2021. The single-shot masterpiece follows the drone flying through the front doors, swooping in and out its nooks and crannies, and soaring down a bowling lane into the pins for a perfect strike. It's the work of local cinematographer Jay Christensen and director Anthony Jaska as part of a project documenting treasured Minnesota businesses suffering due to the pandemic.

Some say Bryant Lake Bowl might be haunted by the ghost of a mechanic who was crushed by a car during the days when the bowling alley was a Model T Ford garage. Look for an apparition of a man in bib overalls and a white T-shirt walking across the vintage lanes.

OLDEST BLACK-OWNED BUSINESS

MINNESOTA SPOKESMAN-RECORDER

3744 S 4th Ave., Mpls. 55409

Five blocks from where police officer Derek Chauvin killed 46-year-old George Floyd by kneeling on his neck for almost 10 minutes on May 25, 2020, stands a cherished emblem of the state's civil rights movement. It's the one-story, mural-covered building that houses the *Minnesota Spokesman-Recorder* (MSR).

The MSR is a weekly, third-generation family newspaper dedicated to elevating the voices of the local African American community. The MSR is not only the state's longest-operating, black-owned business but also one of the longest-standing, family-owned newspapers in the country.

In 1922, at age 17, the newspaper's founder, Cecil Earle Newman, fled his hometown of Kansas City and headed toward Minneapolis with printing press ink pulsing through his veins. Twelve years later, while working as a busboy and Pullman porter, he started not one, but two black newspapers initially in his home: the *Minneapolis Spokesman* and the *St. Paul Recorder*. The two newspapers merged in 2000.

The silver-keyed typewriter on display in the lobby is the same one Newman used for many of his earliest stories and editorials that battled discrimination. According to the

Hennepin History magazine, his front-page editorial on May 10, 1935, triggered a boycott of local breweries after he called them out for not hiring blacks. And his lead story in January 1938 played a critical role in challenging and eventually ending segregated campus housing at the University of Minnesota.

In 1954, Newman built and moved operations into the current building, now a historic landmark adorned with murals promoting themes such as freedom of the press and Black Lives Matter. Newman worked full time until the day he succumbed to a heart attack on February 7, 1976. His widow, Launa Q. Newman, a powerhouse, picked up where he left off. She has since passed away and has a local street named after her. Newman's granddaughter, Tracey Williams-Dillard, took over as CEO/publisher in 2007.

The newspaper's archives reaching back to 1934 can be accessed at the Minnesota Historical Society's digital hub: www.mnhs.org/newspapers/hub.

"I know that the paper makes a difference in people's lives. We are putting light where light needs to be, good or bad." —CEO Tracey Williams-Dillard

Oldest Rose Garden
Lyndale Park Rose Garden

4124 Roseway Rd., Mpls. 55409

One of the prettiest places to savor the change of seasons in the Twin Cities is the Lyndale Park Rose Garden on the northeast corner of Lake Harriet. It's a vibrant world of fragrances, colors, and flower varieties from all over the world. Designed and built by Theodore Wirth, the Rose Garden is the oldest of four themed gardens at Lyndale Park and the second oldest public rose garden in the US.

Wirth started his career as a florist and landscaper in Zurich, London, and Paris. In 1888, he immigrated to the US and created the nation's first municipal rose garden in Hartford, Connecticut. In 1904, as the newly hired superintendent of the Minneapolis Parks System, he set out to create a second one in the Twin Cities.

At the time of Wirth's arrival, Lyndale Park was mostly swamp and woodland. He was intent on creating a rose garden that would be both beautiful and

instructive. With something blooming in every season, it would demonstrate which roses could grow in this climate and how to cultivate them. Completed in 1908, the garden still retains Wirth's original layout of 62 rectangular beds, laid out in classical style. There are more than 3,000 roses representing 250 varieties on display. During its peak season, the garden contains nearly 60,000 blooms.

While strolling through the garden, you'll pass two fountains. The Phelps Fountain, nicknamed the Turtle Fountain, is one of the last remnants of downtown's old Gateway Park. The Heffelfinger Fountain (shown in photo), adorned with decorative Greco-Roman elements, is technically the oldest sculpture in the Minneapolis Park System. Built in the late 1500s for Pope Sixtus V, the fountain originally resided in Fiesole, Italy, before it was purchased in the 1920s by Frank T. Heffelfinger, a prominent figure in early Minneapolis. (Bonus Trivia: His brother is William "Pudge" Heffelfinger, the first athlete to play American football professionally.) Heffelfinger donated the treasured fountain to the Minneapolis Board of Park Commissioners in 1944.

Lyndale Park is home to three other themed gardens as well, including the Annual-Perennial Garden, the Butterfly-Hummingbird Garden, and the Peace Garden, which was designated an International Peace Site on May 5, 1999.

ST. PAUL

Located across from Harriet Island with the High Bridge in the background, St. Paul's Upper Landing Park is a lovely place to stroll along the Mississippi River. It's also where you can grab a beer, eat some good food, and play games inside the 1927 Municipal Elevator and Sackhouse (shown poking out from the trees on the right), a long abandoned grain tower that's now home to City House, a hip eatery and interpretive center.

Oldest State Building
Round Tower at Historic Fort Snelling
200 Tower Ave., St. Paul 55111

In 1805, following the Louisiana Purchase, the US Army sent Lieutenant Zebulon Pike in search of select sites for potential military posts to protect America's interest in the fur trade. When he arrived at Bdote, the center of Dakota spirituality and history at the confluence of the Minnesota and Mississippi Rivers, Pike negotiated a treaty with Dakota representatives.

Although many aspects of that deal remain controversial, it eventually resulted in the Dakota ceding 100,000 acres of their homeland to construct Fort Snelling in 1820, now a National Historic Landmark operated by the Minnesota Historical Society. The fort's earliest surviving structure—a squat, limestone fortress known as the Round Tower—is the oldest Euro-American building in the state. Constructed with defensive rifle slits in the walls, the tower originally served as a guard post but also served many other roles over its history.

In 1919, the tower was converted into a private residence for the fort's electrician, Thomas Marcum, and his family. In a 2015 *Star Tribune* article, one of Marcum's five children, Nina, reminisced about growing up in such a peculiar abode. "It was a lovely home and large enough that you didn't feel like you were living in a circle," she said. After the family moved out in 1938, the Round Tower became a museum dedicated to the fort's history.

Exploring the vast grounds of Fort Snelling today is a visceral connection to stories of both pride and despair. You can learn about the military personnel and domestic slaves who lived there, as well as the fort's secret language school, where Japanese Americans were trained as interpreters and interrogators during World War II. Discover facts about the 1,600 Dakota people corralled during winter months in a prison compound on the riverbank below, following the US-Dakota War of 1862. Many died there while awaiting exile from their homeland, an ugly chapter in Minnesota history still reverberating today.

IF YOU GO: Check www.mnhs.org for the fort's visiting hours and information about their Looking Deeper Walking Tours.

Decommissioned as a military post in 1946, Historic Fort Snelling stands on sacred Dakota homeland, where archeologists have traced human activity as far back as 10,000 years.

——— 8,000 to 10,000 BCE
OLDEST NATURAL SPRING
MNÍ ÓWE SNÍ/COLDWATER SPRING
5601 S Minnehaha Park Dr., St. Paul 55111

Flowing out from layers of limestone bedrock deposited between 425 and 500 million years ago, Coldwater Spring is a beautiful, crystal-clear treasure nestled between Minnehaha Falls and Fort Snelling State Park. Of the four major springs in Hennepin County, Coldwater is the only natural spring remaining.

The site carries strong significance for the Dakota people, whose place name for the spring is *Mní Ówe Sní*. Their people established seasonal villages nearby and have historically used the spring for medicine, purification, washing, and ceremonial uses. Spearpoints and other artifacts have been found in the vicinity, indicating use of the spring by humans dating back 10,000 to 12,000 years ago.

While building Fort Snelling in the 1820s, US soldiers relied on the spring's fresh water as they camped in the surrounding area, known as Camp Coldwater. By 1825, the soldiers had moved into the fort. Soon after, the site began attracting some of the state's first fur traders, missionaries, and blacksmiths. Considered the first settlement in Minnesota that was not primarily a fur trading post, fort, or mission, it was a place where whites and Indigenous people lived alongside each other, intermarrying and conducting trade peacefully for decades.

The water from the spring continued to serve as the primary water source for Fort Snelling until the 1920s, after which the military turned to the city for its water supply. The area surrounding the spring was then abandoned. Eventually, the 27-acre Coldwater campus was turned into the US Bureau of Mines Twin Cities Research Center, until Congress eliminated the center's funding in 1996.

Today, the National Park Service manages the area as a protected historic site and natural park. After walking past the front gate, follow the crushed limestone trail on the far right to the reservoir and stone-walled springhouse, which was built well over a century ago and is surrounded by beautiful trails. See https://bdotememorymap.org for a Dakota perspective about Coldwater Spring and other sacred places.

"Visiting [Mni Ówe Sni] and developing your own relationship to the place will teach you things not found in books or on the Internet. Visit, be quiet and respectful, and your learning will be deeper" (Bdote Memory Map).

Oldest Jewish Deli
Cecil's Deli
651 S Cleveland Ave., St. Paul 55116

Cecil's has that classic New York deli feel you see in the movies. A black-and-white checkered floor leads you to the deli counter. Red-and-white checkered tiles wrap around the upper wall. You can order take-out or casually dine in the small restaurant in the back room, where the walls are covered with old-timey newspaper clippings and family photos.

When Cecil and Faye Glickman first opened Cecil's in 1949, delis serving the vibrant Jewish community of Highland Park were a dime a dozen. But Cecil's is the only one still in operation in that area today. In fact, it's the oldest surviving deli in the state. In 1980, the Glickmans' daughter, Sheila, and her husband, David, purchased the deli. Even then, Cecil would still come in on

Sundays to clean tables and chat with customers. Today, three generations of the family are involved in operations.

The concept of the Jewish deli in America first took root in the mid-1800s when waves of Eastern European immigrants began flocking to New York's Lower East Side. Initially using pushcarts, they peddled their native cured meats and pickled vegetables on the streets. Eventually, they found real estate with countertops and started making ready-to-go, mile-high sandwiches between two slices of rye—and a star was born.

Perusing Cecil's huge, kosher, classic menu is part of the fun. Starters such as matzo ball soup, latkes, and knish come highly recommended. The list of sandwiches, including "The Best Reubens in the Twin Cities," seems endless. Some menu items are named after the grandkids and great-grandkids, like the Sasha, which is a brisket pastrami topped with fried egg, gooey Swiss cheese, and their legendary "zesty bird sauce." The desserts, too, are irresistible, including a few of Faye Glickman's original recipes like the decadent chocolate cake and grasshopper pie.

After grabbing a bite to eat at Cecil's, burn off those calories by exploring nearby Hidden Falls Regional Park or hopping along rocks at the new Uŋči Makhà Park in the Highland Bridge Development (former Ford site).

OLDEST GOLF COURSE
TOWN & COUNTRY CLUB
300 N Mississippi River Blvd., St. Paul 55104

A fter years of decline, the socially distanced sport of golf became a saving grace for countless stir-crazy Minnesotans as the Covid-19 pandemic surged. Throughout the state, we're lucky to have nearly 500 golf courses, some designed by the same architectural giants responsible for America's masterpieces. But the true beginning of golf in these parts was a bit more rudimentary.

The first official round of golf in Minnesota took place in 1893 at St. Paul's Town & Country Club (T&C) on a five-hole course marked by red rags, fishing poles, and tomato cans. According to the club's 100-year anniversary booklet, it all started when a young reporter for the *Saint Paul Dispatch* misquoted charter club member William F. Peet as saying T&C was toying with the idea of adding the game of golf to its amenities. At that time, golf in the US was only beginning to be mentioned in the press along the East Coast.

The next day, George McGree, described by one reporter as "a dynamic, burr-tongued Scotchman with an almost religious reverence for golf" marched into Peet's office and essentially said, "Let's do this!" So the two men lifted a lawn mower into Peet's runabout and cut "the first green ever used for playing golf west of New Jersey." In 1898, T&C formally opened a nine-hole course. In 1906, it became home to the state's first 18-hole

Minnesota's first golf course. Courtesy Town & Country Club

course. Today, it's the second-oldest golf course in the US still being played on its original land, after Shinnecock Hills Golf Club on Long Island.

Incorporated in 1888, T&C was originally located at Lake Como before it relocated to its current home in 1890. It was founded by Nushkas—a social krewe born out of the Winter Carnival and known for wearing "electric blue" fur coats. The most notable among them were Lucius Pond Ordway and James J. Hill. T&C's first official clubhouse, a French-inspired cottage with surrounding verandas, was designed by Minnesota State Capitol architect Cass Gilbert. In 1956, that clubhouse was replaced by the current dark brick clubhouse, now covered in vines.

To learn a little bit more about Minnesota golf history, visit the Minnesota Golf Hall of Fame established in 1987 at Bunker Hills Golf Club in Coon Rapids, featuring a small walkthrough display of legendary trophies, portraits, antique equipment, and memorabilia.

OLDEST CAROUSEL
CAFESJIAN'S CAROUSEL
1245 Midway Pkwy., St. Paul 55103

Tucked inside a million-dollar Victorian pavilion at Como Park, next to the glass-domed Marjorie McNeely Conservatory, is an American treasure straight out of a child's dream. One of the nation's oldest wooden carousels, Cafesjian's Carousel features a Wurlitzer organ, 18 scenery panels, two chariots, and 68 hand-carved horses, no two alike. The story of how it landed in Como Park is nearly as interesting as its extravagant details.

In 1914, entrepreneur Austin McFadden commissioned the Philadelphia Toboggan Company to build the carousel for $8,500. Operated as a concession at the Minnesota State Fair for 75 years, it became a cherished tradition. On November 11, 1988, newspaper headlines announced the carousel's owner had decided to auction off the horses individually to wealthy art collectors. In fact, 20 of the horses were already loaded onto a truck and on their way to an auction in New York.

After hearing the news, a St. Paul couple, Nancy Peterson and Peter Boehm, quickly organized the nonprofit, Our Fair Carousel. With loan backing from the City of St. Paul, the pair traveled to New York. As soon as the auction began and moments before the first of the carousel's horses was about to be sold, they purchased the carousel in its entirety for just over a million dollars.

Soon after, the couple began a fundraising campaign to pay off the loan. Their mailbox filled with letters of support and donations. Nancy and Peter recall one donation in particular from a six-year-old girl named Kim who sent three quarters, two dimes, and a nickel with a note that said, "to save my favorite horse."

The carousel is named for the late Gerard L. Cafesjian, who contributed the majority of the necessary funds to save and restore it. Mr. Cafesjian was an executive with West Publishing Company. He developed an affection for merry-go-rounds while growing up near Coney Island in the 1930s. After the carousel was painstakingly restored, it was initially installed in Town Square in downtown St. Paul. Como Park became its permanent home in 2000.

Courtesy Tamara Beckley

IF YOU GO: For updates on the carousel's operating hours, visit www.ourfaircarousel.org.

About 6,000 wooden carousels were built in the US between 1890 and 1930. About 180 remain; the rest have been abandoned, destroyed by fire or flood, or broken up and sold to collectors. Far fewer are open for public rides.

OLDEST STATE FAIR RIDE

YE OLD MILL
1264 Snelling Ave., St. Paul 55108

Among many local traditions, few are as deeply etched as those upheld at the state fair. "The Great Minnesota Get-Together" has been held every year since 1859 with six exceptions due to wars, the 1946 polio epidemic, and the Covid-19 pandemic.

For some, those traditions include eating every imaginable food on a stick, standing in line for Sweet Martha's chocolate chip cookies, oohing and aahing over baby farm animals,

and witnessing the likeness of dairy princess pageant finalists carved into butter. For love birds, one tradition might include floating in little red boats through the dark channels of Ye Old Mill (aka the Tunnel of Love), the fair's oldest ride at the corner of Underwood Street and Carnes Avenue.

People have been sharing moments of romance, getting engaged, or simply enjoying a brief respite from the heat and crowds in Ye Old Mill's peaceful, winding passages since 1915. Enjoy a four-minute journey as 60,000 gallons of lapping, trickling water carry you into the darkness, past lit-up 3D "vignettes" spotlighting garden gnomes

Courtesy Minnesota State Fair Archives, 1958

and leprechauns, Minnesota north woods, a pot of gold at the end of the rainbow, and fairy-tale favorites.

Designed by the Philadelphia Toboggan Company, Ye Old Mill was constructed out of an old tobacco barn by John Keenan of Oklahoma City. He operated the ride until his death in 1935. His son then took over, and it remained in the Keenan family for five generations. The Keenans at one time owned several other tunnel of love rides around the country, but the Minnesota version is the only survivor. The descendants finally sold the ride for $80,000 to fair officials in 2018.

Don't leave the fair without stopping in at Hamline Dining Hall for some blueberry pancakes, ham loaf, or ice cream. It's the oldest food vendor still in operation at the fair, started by a group of church women in 1897.

OLDEST UNIVERSITY
HAMLINE UNIVERSITY
1536 Hewitt Ave., St. Paul 55104

Conveniently located halfway between Minneapolis and St. Paul, the Hamline-Midway neighborhood is home to the state fairgrounds, the state's first woman-owned microbrewery, a professional soccer stadium, a model railroad museum, and live music venues. It's also home to the honorable Hamline University—Minnesota's oldest institute of higher learning.

Named for Methodist Bishop Leonidas L. Hamline, the private liberal arts college was initially chartered in 1854 in the town of Red Wing. Its first graduating class consisted of two sisters: Emily and Elizabeth Sorin, a monumental achievement considering how few colleges enrolled women at the time. Due to economic turmoil in the years following the Civil War, the school shut down in 1869. After many delays, it reopened in St. Paul in 1880.

The university's most symbolic landmark is Old Main Hall, a Victorian Gothic treasure designed by Minneapolis architect Warren H. Hayes, who was known for his church designs. It was built in 1884 after the first hall burned to rubble the year prior. At that time, it housed the entire university, standing "grim and bare, like a monument in a desert with nothing between it and the North Pole" (*Hamline University: A History*).

Today, Old Main Hall is home to mostly administrative offices, along with the chandeliered Bridgman Auditorium. Look for the portrait of long-ago Hamline president Reverend George Henry Bridgman displayed on the auditorium's wall. Hamline lore alleges the portrait comes alive and Bridgman's spirit wanders around the building some nights.

Mounted on the top of Old Main Hall is a 60-foot, 10-ton clock tower. Up until portions of the clock tower were removed and rebuilt in 1991, the clock was actually painted on. For 106 years, it always read twelve o'clock. In 1915, the tower's manually rung bell was replaced by an electric bell, which was played for the last time when Hamline's football team defeated Gustavus to win the MIAC championship on November 5, 1966. The tower now houses an electric carillon that rings and plays music through loudspeakers. The original bell is carefully stored and brought out each spring at commencement, where it's rung in celebration of the graduates.

While in the area, grab a cup of Thai coffee at Ginkgo Coffeehouse and stroll through the old-growth oak trees of nearby Newell Park, founded in 1901.

Oldest Park Shelter
Hamline Playground Shelter
1564 Lanford Ave., St. Paul 55104

Hard hit by past years of light-rail construction and then the 2020 civil unrest, the Hamline-Midway neighborhood, dubbed "Little Africa," is a survivor. Piece by piece, the community has been coming together to give it a lift.

One of the bright spots is the newly renovated playground at Hamline Park, a wheelchair-accessible fun zone with climbers, slides, swings, bridges, and apparently an imaginary floor that occasionally turns into lava. In contrast, the sandy-colored limestone building next to it is an old beautiful relic of the past.

A 1938 Works Progress Administration project, the building was used as the park's main shelter for 30 years. It was designed by Clarence "Cap" Wigington, the nation's first black municipal architect. Born in Kansas in 1883, Wigington moved to St. Paul in 1914 after gaining experience designing a number of houses, apartments, academic buildings, a church, and a potato chip factory.

Although he was the lead architect in more than 90 St. Paul city projects, Wigington's legacy still does not have the recognition it deserves. Among his showcases are five former St. Paul Winter Carnival ice palaces, Como Park Elementary School, Highland Park Water Tower, Holman Field Administration Building, and Harriet Island Pavilion now named Clarence W. Wigington Pavilion.

Although kids at the playground still run in and out of the former park shelter to use the bathroom, it currently houses an art shop and community studio called Mosaic on a Stick. It's like walking into a sunny garden of green, pink, orange, and red painted walls filled with vibrant stone mosaics.

Mosaic on a Stick is owned by sculptor and artist Lori Green. With a family heritage that's a blend of African and Native American, Greene is driven by a passion for healing art. Her work can be found throughout the Twin Cities, including the nation's first memorial to survivors of sexual violence on Boom Island in Minneapolis. A longtime admirer of Wigington, she jumped at the opportunity to rent this gem when it became available in 2013.

Wigington earned his nickname Cap after he was appointed captain of a Black battalion of the Minnesota Home Guard during World War I.

OLDEST USED BOOKSTORE
MIDWAY USED AND RARE BOOKSTORE
1579 University Ave., St. Paul 55104

For book lovers and collectors, nothing beats the magic, wonder, and earthy scent of a well-worn bookstore. But even the casual reader could spend hours ogling the second-hand and ancient treasures crammed into every crevice inside Midway Used and Rare Books.

Wrapping around an entire block, the store was established in 1965 and is the oldest of the few independent used-book stores still around in the Twin Cities. It's a labyrinth of narrow corridors on three levels holding tens of thousands of used, rare, and collectible books, including the largest art and photography book collection in the Midwest. They also carry vintage magazines and new and collectible comic books. Find the half-door tucked away near the front counter, and descend into the basement packed with gems for $2.50.

About 90 percent of the books are out-of-print, and some of those are extremely rare. One item is the 1634 edition of Italian poet Ludovico Ariosto's epic *Orlando Furioso*, which first appeared in print more than 500 years ago. Another is a page from the

Nuremberg Chronicle dating to 1493. Some have notes and drawings written in the margins or text highlighted with quill pens. Others have gorgeous spines with leather title labels and gold gilt designs.

Current owners Tom and Kathy Stransky, a pair of longtime book lovers who met as teenagers while living in South Minneapolis, purchased the shop in 1980. Their definition of the perfect date back then was the same as it is today: roaming around libraries and bookstores. In fact, they were on a date when they walked into the Midway shop together in the late 1970s, and Tom bought Kathy a five-dollar copy of *Alice in Wonderland* illustrated by Arthur Rackham. Today, the pair travels the country buying and selling rare books at fairs.

While in the Hamline-Midway area, try your luck at vintage arcade games at Can Can Wonderland or stop in at Black Stack Brewery. Both businesses are located inside an 1889 building where Campbell's soup and Spam cans were once manufactured.

OLDEST BLACK CHURCH
PILGRIM BAPTIST CHURCH
732 W Central Ave., St. Paul 55104

The impact of Pilgrim Baptist Church, where the choirs, musicians, praise dancers, and sermons get people clapping and up on their feet, reverberates throughout the Twin Cities. Not only is it a beacon of faith and hope, but it's also a force of outreach that's led to local chapters of the National Association for the Advancement of Colored People, Urban League, Hallie Q. Brown/Martin Luther King Community Center, a prison ministry, food shelf, and more.

Its story begins with Reverend Robert T. Hickman, an enslaved rail-splitter from Boone County, Missouri. Allowed by his owner to learn to read and write, he became a licensed slave preacher. In 1862, at age 32, he escaped slavery, reached the Union Army lines near Jefferson City, and joined the service as a cook in a government hospital. A year later, he returned home to convince a group of 50 or more enslaved men, women, and children to flee north by way of the Underground Railroad. At some point, they constructed a crude raft and headed up the Mississippi River.

After they were discovered adrift by the Union Army, they were towed to St. Paul, arriving on May 6, 1863, where they were met by hostile dockworkers. As a result, they disembarked at Fort Snelling instead. There, they encountered hundreds of Dakota people being held captive in the aftermath of the US–Dakota War of 1862.

Congregation in front of Pilgrim Baptist Church, opening day Dec. 16, 1928.
MNHS Collections

According to Harriet Bishop, moralist and Minnesota's first public school teacher, "The blacks had thought that no mortals were as degraded as themselves but had found themselves outdone."

As these newcomers, who called themselves "Pilgrims," settled into their new lives, they held worship services in individual homes, and then in a rented downtown concert hall. On November 15, 1866, Hickman and others formally organized Pilgrim Baptist Church, making it the oldest predominantly African American Baptist congregation in Minnesota. They celebrated with a baptismal service on the Mississippi River shores. In 1928, the church community moved to its current home in the Rondo neighborhood, a Romanesque building with stained glass windows illuminating the faces of its pioneering Black ministers and Reverend Martin Luther King Jr.

"You can't come to this church and not feel the spirit. I mean, if you walk away and don't have the spirit when you leave, you have to be dead" (Sharon Harper, great-great-granddaughter of Robert T. Hickman, MPR News, 2013).

OLDEST SYNAGOGUE
MOUNT ZION TEMPLE
1300 Summit Ave., St. Paul 55105

Minnesota's first Jewish congregation, known today as Mount Zion Temple, a Reform Jewish community, was founded in 1856 by eight families who had come up the Mississippi River from St. Louis, Missouri. In the early years, services were held in a rented room above a shop on Robert Street between Third and Fourth Streets.

Persecution, poverty, and prejudice sparked multiple waves of Jews to immigrate to the US throughout the 19th and 20th centuries. Jews began making their way to Minnesota with the first wave in the late 1840s. Most pioneer Minnesota Jews were born in Germany.

Construction of Mount Zion's first official temple building, costing $750, began in 1870. It was a modest wooden Gothic Revival building in the Heart of St. Paul's Lowertown retail district at 10th and Minnesota Streets. The second temple, at the same location, costing $11,000, was completed in 1881 in a Moorish style popular at

the time. By 1903, with more than 100 households, Mount Zion built its third temple, costing $80,000.

The 1940s were marked by World War II, the Holocaust, and significant growth for Mount Zion. By 1954, the congregation was once again outgrowing its home, leading to the construction of its fourth (and current) synagogue on Summit Avenue, a million-dollar masterpiece designed by world-renowned architect Erich Mendelsohn. Membership today is well over 600 households.

The synagogue's sanctuary and chapel arks are home to seven scrolls of the Torah, the oldest of which was written roughly 300 years ago. One of those scrolls was rescued from a burning synagogue in Germany. Another survived the Holocaust but only because the Nazis were saving historical materials for "a museum of an extinct race." The congregation commissioned a new Torah for its 150th anniversary in 2006. Used during bar and bat mitzvah ceremonies with each word and letter holding divine meaning, these scrolls are considered tangible embodiments of the heart, mind, and soul of Judaism.

IF YOU GO: Tours for learning more about Judaism are scheduled one hour before the Friday night Shabbat/Sabbath service.

It was the women of Mount Zion Temple who founded the Neighborhood House, which has been a welcoming presence for thousands of refugees and immigrants in St. Paul's West Side since 1897.

OLDEST "NEW" SUPPER CLUB

THE LEXINGTON

1096 Grand Ave., St. Paul 55105

St. Paul's love for the Lexington, that beautiful, stately treasure on historic Grand Avenue, runs deep. One might even say it's the Holy Grail of Twin Cities supper clubs. Push through the heavy front doors, and get ready for a full-on supper club experience.

A typical evening at "the Lex" begins in the plush and welcoming Martini Bar. You can stay and dine there or move to a white-linen-draped table in the Williamsburg dining room, designed to mimic the hull of a luxury ocean liner with wood paneling, chandeliers, and a grand piano for live jazz weekends.

Like any real supper club, there'll be a relish tray, bread rolls, huge and rich dinner portions, and after-dinner ice cream cocktails.

When the Lex was first opened by the McLean family in 1935, it was a sandwich shop inside a drugstore. It quickly became a place where socialites, politicians, and neighborhood folks went to be seen, make business dealings, celebrate milestones, and feel special. One nostalgic customer reminisced to *Mpls.St.Paul Magazine* food writer Stephanie March that his Russian immigrant mother spent her first paycheck on a bowl of soup there just to feel like an American.

After a couple of ownership changes, this neighborhood institution closed in disrepair in 2013, throwing St. Paul off its equilibrium. It was a collective thrill when Smack Shack owners Josh Thoma and Kevin Fitzgerald partnered with legendary local chef Jack Riebel to reopen it in 2017.

While preserving its historical supper club ambience and specialties, such as the famous smoked chicken pot pie, the trio ushered the Lex into the modern age. They updated electrical work, finished the second floor, and added an elevator, banquet rooms, a rooftop patio, a bright row of windows looking into the new kitchen, and an elevated menu with some "new interpretations." Sadly, Chef Jack Riebel, who everybody agrees radiated a special energy, lost his battle with cancer in 2021.

Apparently, there's a fair amount of paranormal activity at the Lex, including chandeliers randomly swinging and apparitions appearing in mirrors. Learn more at their annual Paranormal Cocktail Party each October (tickets sell out very quickly).

OLDEST CURLING ROOTS

ST. PAUL CURLING CLUB

470 Selby Ave., St. Paul 55102

E ven though curling is now a well-established Olympic sport, it still looks, to some, like a bunch of people on ice manically sweeping Swiffer mops to affect the trajectory of a big rock. But to the avid curler, this game, which traces its Scottish roots back to the 1500s, is like chess on ice. Teams battle and strategize for the position of 42-pound stones made from special granites found only in a few locations on Earth.

Polite sportsmanship is key. This often results in the winning team buying the losing team a round of drinks. No wonder its roots run so deep in Minnesota, where there are about 30 curling clubs. One of the most deeply rooted ones is the beloved St. Paul Curling Club (SPCC), which is also the nation's largest with more than 1,500 members.

The first curling match (aka bonspiel) in Minnesota occurred between the SPCC and the brand-new Nushka Club on Christmas Day 1885 on the Mississippi River near Raspberry Island (then called Navy Island). Soon after, the SPCC and other newly formed teams competed during St. Paul's inaugural Winter Carnival dressed in colorful wool coats and knitted caps. Curling has been a highlight at the carnival nearly every year since.

The earlier SPCC hit hard times and folded in 1904. In 1912, the Capital City Curling Club and Nushka Club merged and formed the present-day version of the SPCC. In 1913, the club

opened its current two-story clubhouse tucked into the lovely Cathedral Hill area. Now featuring six sheets of artificial ice, a main-floor club room, a second-floor viewing area with a bar and lounge, and classy wooden lockers emblazoned with images of curling stones, the historic clubhouse has a special place in the minds and hearts of generations of curlers.

IF YOU GO: League games are played Sunday-Friday, 4 p.m. to 11 p.m., from early October to the end of May. Free to spectators.

Within the same neighborhood as the historic clubhouse are numerous treasures, including the St. Paul Cathedral, the Blair Arcade Building that houses the enchanting Nina's Coffee, and W. A. Frost, which is known for its exotic patio and basement that feels like another era.

Oldest Outdoor Sculpture
The New York Life Eagle
418 Summit Ave., St. Paul 55102

The Summit neighborhood is a treasure trove of history and gorgeous old-world mansions. While strolling around, check out the spectacular view of the river valley from the little triangle-shaped Summit Overlook Park at the corner of Summit Avenue and Ramsey Street. That's where you'll meet the *New York Life Eagle*, a one-ton, bronze icon of St. Paul's past.

With a fierce motherly instinct, the eagle's majestic wings are spread while her sharp talons dig into a serpent to protect her nest of eaglets. The form was created in 1890 by Irish-born brothers Augustus and Louis Saint-Gaudens, credited for some of the nation's finest sculptures. Reported in *Ramsey County History* magazine as St. Paul's first outdoor sculpture, the eagle was nearly discarded and forgotten before she was moved to this serene spot in 2004.

She originally adorned the three-story entrance to St. Paul's New York Life Insurance Building, which once stood at Sixth and Minnesota Streets. When that building was destroyed in 1967 to make room for urban development, efforts to save her prompted this headline of the day: "Anybody for a Genuine Homeless Green Eagle?"

Eventually, the rejected raptor was saved from a salvage pile and installed on a lowly pedestal next to the Pioneer Building parking ramp at Fourth and Jackson Streets. After nearly 30 years of neglect, her legal title was secured by Public Art St. Paul. In conjunction with the Ramsey Hill Neighborhood Association, she was restored and moved to her new spot in the shadow of the exclusive University Club.

Once home to the Carpenter Hotel that burned down in the 1880s, Summit Overlook Park had also been long neglected. New landscaping, gravel walkways, and benches have transformed it into a welcoming place. The wrought iron railing was salvaged from the old Selby Avenue Bridge. The retaining wall is embedded with stones from the old High Bridge demolished in 1985. Several plaques detail the site's history.

St. Paul's Summit Avenue is the longest stretch of Victorian mansions remaining in the country. The oldest of them is located at 312 Summit Avenue, built in 1858. Learn colorful tales about this historic neighborhood on walking tours led by the Minnesota Historical Society (mnhs.org).

——————————————————1887

OLDEST
CZECH-SLOVAK HALL
C.S.P.S. HALL
383 Michigan St., St. Paul 55102

I t's been said that Czechs carry a bit of their homeland wherever they go. There's no place in Minnesota where that's more true than inside the Czech-Slovak Protective Society Hall (C.S.P.S.).

Built in 1887, the C.S.P.S. Hall is the longest-serving national hall in Minnesota as well as the longest-serving Czech-Slovak hall in continuous use in the US.

During scheduled events, the center buzzes with a wide range of activities from gymnastics competitions and language classes to candlelight roast duck dinners and performances of lavishly dressed dancers stomping their feet to polka music. The three-level hall, available to rent for special events, includes a gymnasium/theater featuring a stage with six backdrops that evoke scenes of native Bohemia, painted by Victor Hubal in the 1920s.

The focal point of activities held inside the historic hall is the Czech and Slovak Sokol Minnesota. Sokol was an international movement founded in Prague in 1862 by Dr. Miroslav Tyrš to encourage community and fitness through physical, educational, cultural, and social programs. The word *Sokol* means falcon, a bird symbolizing an active, vigorous, strenuous, and independent life.

Sibrinky Dancers, St. Paul Sokol, 1941.
MNHS Collections

From the mid-1800s to the early 1900s, Czechs migrated to the US in increasingly large numbers. They were followed by a mass movement of Slovaks from the 1880s through the First World War. The St. Paul-based Sokol, a fraternal organization, became very popular and inspired the creation of Sokols throughout the Midwest.

A mile east of the C.S.P.S. is High Bridge Park, where an assortment of artwork honors the Czech and Slovak immigrants who have lived in the West End of St. Paul since the 1860s.

OLDEST LAGER SALOON
WALDMANN BREWERY & WURSTERY
445 Smith Ave., St. Paul 55102

Along a busy avenue near the High Bridge stands a stately limestone time capsule operating as Waldmann Brewery. In the years leading up to the Civil War, this is where German immigrants, often entire families, gathered around tables to play games, gossip, smoke cigars and pipes, snack on pigs' feet and pretzels, and drink cold lager beer in small wooden rooms lit up by lamps burning whale oil.

After hundreds of hours of research, owner Tom Schroeder traced the building's past to 1857. It was first inhabited by Bavarian immigrants Anton and Wilhelmina Waldmann. While living upstairs, the couple operated a saloon downstairs until 1864. After they moved out, it was transformed into a private home for 123 years as its earliest chapter faded into memory.

Schroeder—an attorney, historian, and home brewer—first started noticing the building in 1992. It had become a "vacant wreck" by the time he bought the property for restoration purposes in 2008. While Schroeder and architect John Yust began digging on-site, they found treasures, including bottles, dishes, a rare beer token, and a stencil reading "A. Waldmann."

The biggest discovery of all, though, were records found within Minnesota Historical Society archives showing the building's original purpose as a lager saloon—a special breed back in the day. Because the temperance community, which was against the sale of alcohol, believed that lager had less alcohol (it doesn't, according to Waldmann's website), city ordinances exempted them from paying liquor license fees and taxes. Once part of a cluster of 30 or more in the area, Waldmann Brewery is not only the oldest lager saloon still standing in the area but also the oldest commercial building in the entire city.

Reopened in 2017, Waldmann Brewery glows with restored details of the mid-1800s, such as woodstoves, virgin pine doors and floors, handblown glass windows, steamboat chairs, old maps, and paraffin lamps. Outside is a new barn for brewing operations and a Biergarten with heaters, fire rings, and picnic tables. It's a beautiful and friendly place to enjoy some "Wurst und Bier" year-round.

"This is a time-travel opportunity that exists in only a few places in the country . . . It's a fabulous place to sit and just take in the atmosphere."—Tom Schroeder (Pioneer Press, *July 19, 2014*).

OLDEST FIREHOUSE
1872
HOPE BREAKFAST BAR
1 S Leech St., St. Paul 55102

In a world that often feels broken, there's Hope Breakfast Bar, across from Children's Hospital in the historic West Seventh neighborhood. Opened in 2019, the two-story café, swirling with an inviting mix of aromas from chocolate pancakes to pork belly tacos, is housed inside St. Paul's oldest remaining firehouse.

Originally known as Hope Engine Company No. 3., the firehouse was constructed in 1872 by volunteer firefighters. Yes, the fireman pole is still there. No, you can't slide down it. Why? Because it's anchored from upstairs right through the center of one of the lower-level dining tables.

The structure served as St. Paul's first volunteer fire station in operation until 1956. In 2016, it was scheduled for demolition to make way for a new hotel. Fortunately, neighborhood groups

prevailed to save this piece of history. During renovations, the US flag now on display upstairs was found inside the walls.

This friendly spot has all the positive vibes. The front door is propped open on nice days with a fire hydrant. The French toast is whitewashed with cotton candy. Their St. Paul mule has the perfect amount of applejack brandy. The booths are made from repurposed church pews. In 2022, a second Hope Breakfast Bar opened in St. Louis Park.

Hope Breakfast Bar is part of a collection of purpose-driven restaurants owned by Brian and Sarah Ingram (see www.purposerestaurants.com). "Hope Cards" are placed on every table for customers to write down hopes, dreams, and prayer requests. The Ingrams say they read every single card that's turned in to learn about crises in the community that could benefit from their nonprofit—Give Hope MN.

Since its opening, Hope Breakfast Bar has weathered a pandemic, served as a free community kitchen and food bank, raised funds to support the families of victims of gun violence, and fed health-care workers, protesters, and the unemployed.

————————————1849
OLDEST NEIGHBORHOOD
IRVINE PARK
281 Walnut St., St. Paul 55102

Almost hidden in the shadows of downtown, just a few blocks from the Xcel Energy Center, is the magical time capsule of Irvine Park, St. Paul's oldest neighborhood.

Streets lined with restored pre-Civil War homes radiate out from a park reminiscent of a New England–style public square with a gazebo and ornate water fountain. Some days, the park is so quiet that it feels like a secret. Other days, it's bustling with brides and grooms and prom dates posing for photographs.

After this area was first donated by shipping titan John Irvine in 1849, it quickly became the "It" neighborhood, where some of the city's early leading citizens lived in high fashion. Among the first were Alexander Ramsey and his wife, Anna. Ramsey, whose impact on the state is muddied due to his role in the removal of the Dakota people, served as Minnesota's first territorial governor and second state governor. Their home at 265 Exchange Street is now owned by the Minnesota Historical Society.

Every home surrounding the park has a story to tell. The French Revival at 59 Irvine Park was built for Dr. Justus Ohage, who performed the country's first successful gall bladder operation and opened the city's first zoo at Harriet Island. The mansion (and former restaurant) at 276 Exchange Street South, built for Joseph Forepaugh, is supposedly haunted by the ghost of a young maid, Molly, who hanged herself in the 1880s. The refurbished abode at 234 Ryan Avenue, built for sea captain Charles Symonds in 1850, is mentioned in many sources as St. Paul's oldest remaining house.

Following the Great Depression, the neighborhood fell into a gradual decline. In 1978, grassroots preservationists secured historic status for the neighborhood. The dilapidated houses were offered for one dollar to buyers willing to bring them up to code. Historic homes were transported in from other parts of the city, and a park fountain was built for $40,000 to closely match the original, which had been scrapped for metal.

Near the neighborhood entry at 217 Chestnut Street, look for the small Cossetta Park marked by a Charlie Brown statue, Charlie Andiamo Americano, *which commemorates the area's early-day Italian immigrants.*

OLDEST ITALIAN MARKET
COSSETTA ALIMENTARI
211 W 7th St., St. Paul 55102

For all the smells, tastes, and bright colors of Italy right here in the Twin Cities, step past the green awning into Cossetta Alimentari. What was once a tiny food market with standing room for a handful of people is now a full-sensory adventure within a 40,000-square-foot, three-story emporium, owned and operated by the family's fourth generation.

In the late 1800s, Michael Cossetta immigrated to Minnesota and settled in St. Paul's "Upper Landing" area, once a steamboat docking port bustling with immigrants. In 1911, he opened his food market, which quickly became a cornerstone for the community. Eventually, Michael's son, Frank, took over operations. Although Frank stood less than five feet tall, he had a giant's heart like his father, never turning anyone away who was hungry or short on cash.

The Cossetta of today is like a mini museum. Historic photos cover the walls and boast of celebrities who have dined there, from Frank Sinatra and Henry Winkler to Alan Page and Katie Couric. Newspaper clippings tell the story of the immediate West Seventh

Cossetta in 1952. Courtesy Cossetta and MNHS Collections

neighborhood, home to several other legendary establishments, such as Mancini's Char House and the Schmidt Brewery complex.

Through Cossetta's front doors, a two-story eatery and pizzeria are unveiled, where you can grab a tray and move through the line. A few steps away is the Italian food market that started it all, now three times its original size with a great assortment of Italian breads, cheeses, meats, and hard-to-find imported ingredients. Adjacent to that is a pastry shop built from marble shipped piece-by-piece from Tuscany, complete with chandeliers. Latest additions include an Italian street-food bar called Frank's Levee Tavern on the second floor. And for a fine-dining rooftop experience, climb the mahogany stairs one more floor to Louis Ristorante & Bar.

Cossetta Alimentari stands on West Seventh Street, Minnesota's oldest commercial corridor. Originally known as Fort Road, it was a historic Native American and fur-trading path from downtown St. Paul to Fort Snelling.

OLDEST CULTURAL INSTITUTION
MINNESOTA HISTORICAL SOCIETY
345 W Kellogg Blvd., St. Paul 55102

I f you really want to plunge into Minnesota's past, explore the Minnesota History Center, a 470,000-square-foot landmark constructed to match the grandeur of the nearby State Capitol and St. Paul Cathedral. It contains an award-winning museum, the renowned Gale Family Library, and a behind-the-scenes treasure trove of objects, books, and historic materials curated by the Minnesota Historical Society (MNHS).

Establishing the MNHS was one of the first acts of the first session of the Minnesota Territorial Legislation. Since 1849, its staff and volunteers have been collecting and preserving Minnesota's stories in all their forms, from letters, photographs, and newspapers to artwork and artifacts dating back more than 9,000 years.

Prior to the construction of the Minnesota History Center in 1992, the MNHS occupied what's now the Minnesota Judicial

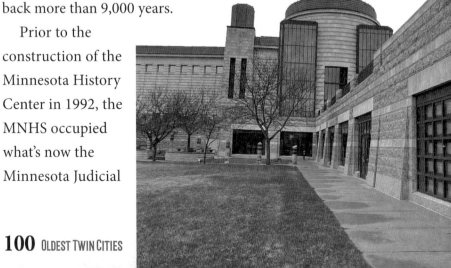

Center. Before that, it was housed in the basement of the State Capitol. Today, it's the largest state history organization in the nation, encompassing 26 historical sites and museums, a nonprofit publishing company, education outreach services, archeology programs, and historical preservation resources.

Charge your senses while exploring the Minnesota History Center and appreciating local symbolism incorporated into artwork on the ceilings, floors, and entryway doors. You can board a street car, sit quietly in a teepee, walk through a mud home, relive a historic tornado, experience a 1930s movie theater, sit at a classic soda fountain, or listen to stories about soldiers who risked their lives for freedom.

Check out the dramatic view of the State Capitol from the large picture windows on the third floor of the Great Hall. The Quadriga located at the base of the Capitol Dome, officially known as *Progress of the State,* is a four-horse chariot gilded in six pounds of gold leaf. And don't forget to take a selfie in front of the giant Minnesota postcard before you leave.

IF YOU GO: Open Wednesday through Sunday. Admission ranges from $8 to $12. Digital MNHS archives can be accessed at www.mnhs.org/research.

According to its website, the Minnesota Historical Society, housed inside the Minnesota History Center, manages more than 250,000 objects, 6,000 works of art, 100,000 cubic feet of paper records, 300,000 photographs, half a million books, 3 million feet of news film, and much more.

Oldest Public Square
Rice Park
109 W 4th St., St. Paul 55102

L ocated against a backdrop of architectural and cultural giants, Rice Park adds a touch of old-world European charm to downtown. It was once a pasture used for grazing sheep and cleaning rugs. Today, it's a 1.6-acre treasure of violas, globe lanterns, diagonal pathways, and whimsical sculptures.

Rice Park was the first of three public squares created in 1849. The other two were Irvine Park and Smith Park (now Mears Park). It's named after Minnesota's first US senator, Henry Mower Rice, who donated the land with assistance from St. Paul banker John Irvine. Seven years older than New York's Central Park, Rice Park has been the go-to spot for many notable events, including a huge celebration to mark the completion of the Northern Pacific Railroad's line to the West Coast in 1883, women's suffrage rallies, new soldier recruit assemblies, US presidential speeches, parades, jazz concerts, and St. Paul Winter Carnival ice sculpture contests.

The St. Paul Women's Institute and St. Paul Garden Club raised funds for renovation in 1964, adding the park's centerpiece, Alonzo Hauser's *The Source*, which is a fountain with a statue of a woman in a ballet pose. The park was renovated again in 2019 by the St. Paul Garden Club, St. Paul Parks Conservancy, and Rice Park Association.

At the northeast corner stands a bronze sculpture honoring the city's most venerated author F. Scott Fitzgerald looking dapper in his 30s. Facing Fourth Street are Peppermint Patty kicking a football and Marcy reading on a bench with Woodstock looking over her shoulder, an ode to St. Paul's Charles Schulz. The rest of the core Peanuts gang are hanging out at the Landmark Plaza adjacent to Rice Park.

Prominent buildings bordering the park include the 1917 Downtown Central Library, the 1902 Landmark Center (former Federal Courts Building), the 1985 Ordway, and the 1910 St. Paul Hotel, where countless prominent guests have slept and dined, from gangsters, authors, and aviators to movie stars, rock 'n' roll legends, and world leaders.

Rice Park is especially magical in the winter with its twinkly ice rink. It has been the longtime anchor for the St. Paul Winter Carnival, the nation's oldest (and weirdest) winter festival, dating back to 1886.

Oldest Downtown Building
Original Coney Island Tavern and Café
448 St. Peter St., St. Paul 55102

While the downtown area around it keeps evolving, the Original Coney Island venue stands like a vestige of another era. Step inside, and you're transported to the 1930s with the original tin ceilings, wooden booths, penny scale, mahogany art deco bar, and a jukebox that plays

songs like "Ol' Man River" by Frank Sinatra and "Over the Rainbow" by Judy Garland.

The two-building complex was restored by the founding family in 2001 and is now a designated landmark. The shorter of the two buildings at 448 St. Peter Street dates back to 1858, making it the oldest commercial structure downtown. It once served as an armory during the Civil War.

Nicholas Arvanitis, who immigrated to St. Paul from Greece, converted the complex

into the Original Coney Island Tavern and Café in 1923 after fighting in World War I and earning US citizenship. While cooking up those signature hot dogs smothered with onions, mustard, and secret sauce, Nicholas and his wife, Frances, raised six children. When Nicholas died, Frances and their two sons, Louie and Harry, continued the business. That is, until one day, in 1994, a "Closed for Today" sign was posted in the window. Frances had fallen ill, and her children rallied to care for her.

Although it's no longer open on a daily basis, the nostalgic structure is operated as a special events center, managed by owner Mary Arvanitis, the youngest of Nick and Frances's children. Locals can still experience its historic atmosphere during private gatherings, vintage city tours operated through the Landmark Center, and public events, such as its annual opening during the St. Paul Winter Carnival's Torchlight Parade. Follow the Original Coney Island Restaurant and Bar Facebook page for those rare public events.

The ambience of the Original Coney Island venue evokes a vision of John Dillinger from St. Paul's early 1900s gangster days emerging from the shadows, sporting a fedora hat, striped vest, and pocket watch.

—1939

OLDEST RAILCAR DINER
MICKEY'S DINER
36 W 7th St., St. Paul 55102

A guidebook about historic treasures in the Twin Cities wouldn't be complete without Mickey's Diner, one of the most historic diners in the country, built to resemble a vintage railcar. This nationally known diner has been featured in a handful of Hollywood movies, including *Mighty Ducks* and *Jingle All the Way*, and in publications such as *Smithsonian*, *National Geographic*, and *Sports Illustrated*.

After an extended hiatus, first due to the pandemic, then restorations, repairs, and delays, the reopening of this iconic landmark was still uncertain as this book went into final

production. Prior to that, it had continuously served greasy-spoon food, hangover coffee, and thick malts 'round the clock, 365 days a year, at the same location for nearly 80 years. You could practically smell the history sizzling on the old cast-iron griddle.

David "Mickey" Crimmons and John "Bert" Mattson opened Mickey's in 1939. Shipped to St. Paul on a flatbed railcar, the 50-foot by 10-foot structure was manufactured by the Jerry O'Mahony Diner Company of New Jersey. There was a time when such diners could be found throughout every city in America. Now, only a handful remain. While most of them had plain white exteriors, Mickey's has its own art deco charm accentuated by a bright red and cream streamline design, earning it a spot in the National Register of Historic Places.

The scene inside was once described by *City Pages* as "a dollop of Edward Hopper Americana." You can sit in one of four laminated booths adorned with mini tabletop jukeboxes, or at one of the red swivel stools lined up in front of a long counter. There you can catch up on local buzz while watching beads of sweat roll down the cook's neck as he whips up fluffy omelets and pancakes, O'Brien potatoes, grilled sandwiches, and homemade mulligan stew to perfection.

"Mickey's is the kind of place that you need when things are rough and the night is cold … It isn't the kind of place you go to impress a date or show off the high culinary skills of the Twin Cities. Take it for what it is, and you will have a five-star experience."
—Customer Review

OLDEST ART MUSEUM
MINNESOTA MUSEUM OF AMERICAN ART
350 N Robert St., St. Paul 55101

While some cultural institutions went dark as the pandemic began to wreak havoc, others found ways to stay connected with their audiences, primarily through digital offerings. The Minnesota Museum of American Art, a treasure trove of American artists from the 19th century to the present, brought its art and storytelling to the community through displays in the Jackson Street skyway and animated window galleries between Fourth and Fifth Streets.

Courtesy Peter J. Sieger
Architectural Photography

"The M," as locals call it, has always been more than a physical place, though, and is all too familiar with reinventing itself. Founded as the St. Paul School of Fine Arts in 1894, it's the state's oldest visual arts organization and has operated under seven names and from more than 13 different venues throughout its history. The museum even found itself homeless for several years starting in 2009.

In 2018, the museum moved into its new permanent home—the two-story lobby of the 1889 Pioneer Building,

which was uniquely linked with the L-shaped Endicott Building like a geometric puzzle in the 1940s. The M's collection of 5,000 artworks, including sculptures, paintings, drawings, photographs, and studio crafts is one of great breadth and depth. At the heart of it are local artists who labored in this region and artworks that represent diverse perspectives. The interior gallery plans to reopen in late 2023. Upon completion of its planned expansion phases, the museum will cover 36,000 square feet.

IF YOU GO: Check out the Pioneer Building's historic 16-story light court and open-cage elevators. Also, don't miss the opportunity to try a hand-dipped truffle at Legacy Chocolates Cafe right above the museum.

In its early years, the Pioneer Building, which houses the museum, was home to Minnesota's first newspaper, first glass elevator, first commercial radio station, and one of the world's first telephone answering services.

OLDEST THEATER SPACE
FITZGERALD THEATER
10 E Exchange St., St. Paul 55101

Nowhere in the world are there more tributes to the late, great author F. Scott Fitzgerald than in St. Paul.

After all, St. Paul is where Fitzgerald—known for portraying the lavishness of the Jazz Age in his novels, especially in *The Great Gatsby*—was born, became a writer, and socialized among the grand homes of Summit Hill before leaving for more luxurious destinations. So, it's no surprise to see a huge portrait of him staring down from the side of St. Paul's oldest surviving theater space, which now bears his name.

Standing on the corner of Exchange and Wabasha Streets like a "grand old elegant lady," the Fitzgerald Theater, known locally as "the Fitz," was hailed as one of the most beautiful theaters of its day. Today, it's one of a rare breed, featuring three tiers of seating, two balconies,

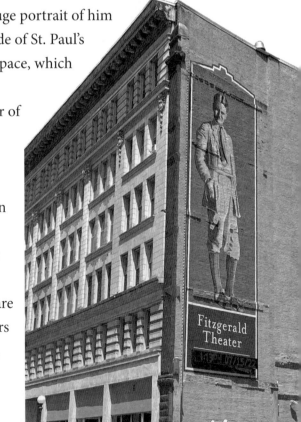

red plush seats, a burgundy velour stage curtain, and eight curved opera boxes adorned with glittering gold leaf. With near-perfect acoustics and sight lines, there's not a bad seat in the house.

The venue was first established as the Sam S. Shubert Theater in 1910 by entertainment industry leaders Lee and J. J. Shubert, who named it in honor of their brother who died in a train wreck. The brothers also opened a theater in Minneapolis with the same name (now the Goodale Theater at the Cowles Center). In 1933, the St. Paul theater was converted into a foreign-film house and renamed the World Theater.

Minneapolis Public Radio purchased and rehabbed the building in the 1980s. Under their ownership, it became the stage for Garrison Keillor's *A Prairie Home Companion* live radio broadcast, featuring talented musicians and comedians, as well as Keillor's own comedic skits about a fictional Minnesota town, Lake Wobegon. In 1994, Keillor petitioned to rename the theater in honor of the St. Paul–born author. Since 2019, the theater has been owned and operated by Minneapolis's legendary music club First Avenue, which is committed to continuing the Fitzgerald's cultural, literary, and musical legacy with Broadway shows, concerts, and lectures.

Some believe the Fitz is haunted by a former stagehand named Ben, who allegedly moves tools around, and a former actress named Veronica, whose singing voice sometimes echoes in the auditorium at night.

OLDEST SPORTING CLUB
MINNESOTA BOAT CLUB
1 S Wabasha St., St. Paul 55107

I n the early morning, while the rest of the city is still sleeping, members of the Minnesota Boat Club (MBC) slip into long, narrow rowing boats called shells and push off from

the shores of Raspberry Island. As they head upstream to log some hours, their oars scuttle and sweep across the sparkling surface of the Mississippi River in a smooth, rhythmic motion. The energy is seriously magical.

Raspberry Island, a former navy training site, is a two-acre gem of tranquility beneath the Wabasha Street Bridge. You can access it from Harriet Island or by the bridge's winding staircase. On the western portion is where you can view MBC's 1910 Spanish Revival rock and stucco boathouse with an impressive storage room of shells and an upstairs chandelier ballroom for special events. This replaced the club's original boathouse, which was wooden and prone to flooding.

Founded in 1870, MBC was the first formal athletic organization in Minnesota. It all started in 1868 when John W. L. Corning, an avid rower who had relocated from Brooklyn to St. Paul, launched his single rowing shell, made of shellacked paper, into the river. A crowd gathered on the Wabasha Street Bridge to watch, thrilled to see the national rowing craze had finally arrived in their town. Two years later, MBC was founded with Corning among its first 10 members.

In 1874, the club hosted its first annual intra-club Fourth of July regatta. Before long, the club was producing highly competitive racers and gaining a national reputation. By the 1890s, though, people became more interested in tennis and golf. Competitive rowing in the Twin Cities came to a halt until it picked up speed again in the early 1900s. Today, the club offers competitive and recreational rowing at every level.

Raspberry Island is also home to a unique bandshell. Commissioned by the historic Schubert Club and Public Art St. Paul in 2002, its curvy glass and steel design echoes the waves along the river.

1964
OLDEST MEXICAN EATERY
BOCA CHICA
11 Cesar Chavez St., St. Paul 55107

L ocated in District del Sol in West St. Paul, Boca Chica centers around a family legacy that translates to Mexican food royalty in Minnesota. But the moment you walk through the front door of this neighborhood landmark, you know this is more than a place to enjoy Grandma Frías's homemade seasoned pork tamales.

Adorned in family photographs, cultural artifacts, colorful fireplaces, and murals representing centuries of legends and bullfighting, the whole place is a celebration of the founding family's heritage. The story of Boca Chica began when Guillermo Frías immigrated to America and fell in love with Gloria Coronado, a petite, no-nonsense woman linked to a local cultural dynasty.

Gloria's parents, Arturo and Elvira Coronado, opened Minnesota's first Mexican restaurant, La Casa Coronado. It was first located in St. Paul, then in Minneapolis, and now long gone. After Guillermo and Gloria married, they opened

a little cantina of their own with seating for 28 in 1964. They named it Boca Chica after a small town on the Gulf of Mexico, where Guillermo spent time as a child. Translated, it means "little mouth of the river."

In between attending their kids' baseball games, Guillermo and Gloria created the menu for Boca Chica, gradually introducing the Twin Cities to unfamiliar flavors of stews, sauces, and *sopes* of Mexico. The Frías also began hosting educational seminars for Spanish-language students at the restaurant. Eventually, Guillermo and Gloria's son, Alfredo, took over management of the cantina. Nicknamed Freddie, he ushered the restaurant into a new era.

Under Freddie's leadership, the restaurant was expanded to include a full bar, patio, and three dining rooms where every wall tells a story. As one of the founders of the area's annual Cinco de Mayo festival, Freddie was deeply vested in his community. School groups would come in to sample food and listen to him talk about the culture. Then he'd teach them how to make salsa tortillas. Alfredo died of heart complications in 2018 at age 63. The third generation of the Frías family, primarily Alfredo's son and daughter, José and Jesie, now carry on the legacy and traditions.

The little balcony above Boca Chica's front entrance symbolizes a pivotal moment in Mexican history. In 1810, Fr. Miguel Hidalgo y Costilla stepped out onto a parish balcony in the village of Delores to call for a revolution, instigating the Mexican War of Independence against Spain.

—— AT LEAST 8,000 BCE
OLDEST CITED CAVE
WAKAN TIPI/CARVER'S CAVE
265 Commercial St., St. Paul 55106

Exploring the Bruce Vento Nature Sanctuary, a 27-acre oasis located just east of downtown at the base of 450-million-year-old bluffs, is like stepping into a different world.

Before it was desecrated in the mid-1800s for industrial use, this site was a vibrant floodplain, where Minnesota's native inhabitants lived, held ceremonies, and buried loved ones in nearby mounds.

The first European known to have visited this site was Jonathan Carver, a mapmaker who lived with the Dakota people there in 1766–1767.

In his journals, Carver describes a "Great Cave." He writes about a lake within the cave and extensive rock art at its entrance, representing ancient stories and spirituality. Carver's account is the first published documentation of a cave in the Midwest. To many, it's known as Carver's Cave. But its original Dakota name is *Wakan Tipi*, "Dwelling of the Great Spirit."

The cave prior to removal of the original entrance, est. 1875, MNHS Collections

The cave as it appears today, nearly hidden across from a pond and protected by a steel gate.

Tucked into the bluffs with fresh water still trickling from it, the cave is located at the far east end of the sanctuary, across from a pond. Now in the National Register of Historic Places, it's protected with a steel gate. (You'll first pass by the gated North Star Brewery Cave, which is easier to view.) The petroglyphs were destroyed after Wakan Tipi's original entrance was blasted to make room for a railroad. The surrounding wetlands were filled in, trees removed, and the soil, air, and water contaminated. When the railroads declined, the area turned into an unofficial wasteland.

Thanks to the Lower Phalen Creek Project, a Native American–led coalition, this storied landscape is slowly being restored. Glimpses of spring-fed ponds, cottonwoods, and soaring songbirds stir the imagination of what it once was. See www.lowerphalencreek.org for updates about the development of the Wakan Tipi Center, scheduled to open on the grounds in Spring 2024.

Above the cave and bluffs is Indian Mounds Regional Park, where you'll find six prehistoric burial mounds (dozens more were razed by developers) believed to have been constructed by Hopewell Native Americans 2,000 years ago.

OLDEST BREWERY REBORN
YOERG BREWING COMPANY
378 Maria Ave., St. Paul 55106

I f you haven't already heard, you'll be happy to know the formulas created by Minnesota's first brewery, the long-lost Yoerg Brewing Company, have been dusted off in recent years. Better yet, that legendary brewery has been brought back to life in the form of a picturesque neighborhood taproom on Dayton's Bluff.

Anthony Yoerg immigrated to St. Paul from the Bavarian village of Gundelfingen when he was 19. He began brewing German beer out of his home and delivering it to neighbors by wheelbarrow. As demand grew, Yoerg built a brewery in 1848 near what is today the Xcel Energy Center. Two decades later, Yoerg expanded into an extensive stone brewery across the Mississippi River. The business closed in 1952 after Yoerg's last surviving son passed away and historic flooding stopped production.

Thanks to St. Paul resident Thomas Keim, the Yoerg brand has been resurrected. Keim's fascination with the brand formed as a young boy while working at his father's liquor store in the 1960s. "It was my job to sort through the returnable bottles in the basement," Keim said. When Keim found a box of Yoerg bottles, he couldn't identify them, so he showed them to his dad, who said, "They went out of business. Just throw them out." Enamored by the cool artwork on the bottles, Keim did what he was told but kept one for himself.

Keim eventually secured rights and began perfecting recipes from the family's paperwork. In 2018, he and his business partner, Carole Minogue, turned an 1885 Victorian structure, formerly Strip Club Meat & Fish, into a re-creation of Yoerg Brewing Company. It's a cozy, retro nano-brewery with the sounds of Frank Sinatra and Dean Martin playing in the background. They also offer a wide selection of European imports, artisan wines, and old-world menu items.

Yoerg's Brewery was truly a family operation. Anthony Yoerg's wife, Elovina Seitzsinger, whom he met while she was a nanny for Governor Alexander Ramsey, took part in the operations as did their seven children.

Oldest Family Italian Restaurant
Yarusso-Bros Italian Restaurant
635 Payne Ave., St. Paul 55130

There's no better place in the Twin Cities to soak up local history while feasting on spaghetti and giant meatballs than Yarusso's, a cornerstone of the Payne-Phalen neighborhood since the Great Depression. You might even hear faint echoes of the past floating up from the steep, hidden valley across the street, known as Swede Hollow, home to the city's poorest immigrants for nearly a century.

The restaurant's founder, Francesco Yarusso, was born in a small village south of Rome. In 1899, he immigrated to New Jersey, where he met and married Dora Corbo. In 1904, the couple moved to St. Paul. Eventually, they had 14 children. Their first home was a shanty in Swede Hollow before moving "up the hill" in 1919. "The Hollow" was where many of the first Swedish, Polish, Italian, and Latino immigrants made a life for themselves after arriving in the city. In 1956, the area was deemed a health hazard and burned down by city officials. Today, it's a serene nature preserve.

In 1933, Francesco and Dora opened a tavern, and then expanded it into Square Deal Café, which was renamed Yarusso's in 1947 when their children took over. The family installed St. Paul's first bocce ball alleys outside the building,

which have since been removed. Men from Swede Hollow with nicknames like Chili Joe, Peewee, and Moon Face would climb up the hill to play the Italian sport while smoking pipes and cigars. Later, their wives would send the children up the hill to tell the men to come home. "I still remember the smell of the restaurant. It was pipe smoke, cigar smoke, and spaghetti sauce," Bob DePalma reminisced to the *Pioneer Press*.

Today, the restaurant is operated by the third and fourth generations of Yarussos. Displayed on its dark paneled walls are historic photos and art, including dramatic paintings of Swede Hollow and the Rome Colosseum.

To access Swede Hollow from Yarusso's, go up half a block on Payne Avenue, take a right on Preble Street, and then take a quick left on Beaumont Street. On the left is a small sign indicating entrance to Swede Hollow. Follow the sidewalk down through the historic tunnel to reach Swede Hollow, now part of the Bruce Vento Trail.

OLDEST ROUNDHOUSE
JACKSON STREET ROUNDHOUSE
193 E Pennsylvania Ave., St. Paul 55130

The city of St. Paul prospered in large part because of the railroad industry and James J. Hill, a dazzling, quick-tempered tycoon whose entrepreneurial legacy throughout the Twin Cities and the country is nothing short of phenomenal. His 1891 mansion still stands on Summit Avenue as a museum.

One of Hill's greatest contributions was the transcontinental Great Northern Railway, running from St. Paul to Seattle. In 1889, Hill opened a 32-acre maintenance facility, known as the Jackson Street Shops, where passenger trains were repaired, washed, greased, oiled, and stored for their next assignment inside a circular structure called a roundhouse. Locomotives were moved around to their assigned stall in the engine house or railyard by a turntable. All that remains of Hill's shops today are the stone buildings west of Jackson Street Bridge, including a second roundhouse, built in 1907.

The 1907 roundhouse was decommissioned in 1959. However, it's still fully functional as the maintenance facility for the Osceola and St. Croix Valley Railway and is one of the last of its kind in the country. It's also now part of the Minnesota Transportation Museum, a treasure trove of railway history for the whole family.

The museum is home to railway memorabilia, locomotives, and passenger cars that still look like they did while crossing

America over a century ago with plush seating, lanterns, ornate woodwork, and sleeping quarters. There's also a maintenance shop and an authentic blacksmith shop. On Saturdays, admission includes a ride through the railyard on a 100-year-old caboose.

IF YOU GO: The museum is open year-round on Wednesdays and Saturdays from 10 a.m. to 4 p.m. Check www.transportationmuseum.org to learn about train rides they offer in the St. Croix River Valley.

The Jackson Street Roundhouse is run by hundreds of volunteers, from retired lawyers to veteran railroaders. Through hands-on training provided by the museum, they become real conductors and railyard masters.

OLDEST CEMETERY
OAKLAND CEMETERY
927 Jackson St., St. Paul 55117

O akland Cemetery, the oldest in the Midwest, is more than a tranquil place to pay homage to departed loved ones. It's a place of beauty to be savored and enjoyed. Visitors stroll amid oak groves, winding paths, and posthumous sculptures that render the cemetery akin to an outdoor museum.

In 1853, civic leaders responded to demands for a large nonsectarian cemetery by initially purchasing 40 acres of land north of the current State Capitol. A standard seven-by-three-foot burial plot sold for $3.15. Prior to that, "the town had a few church bone yards but no place for the differently-churched, the unchurched, paupers, and visitors to be buried" (*MNopedia*).

Designed by Horace W. S. Cleveland, one of the great landscape architects of the 19th century, Oakland is the final resting place for many of the city's founders and most prominent citizens. Among them are Minnesota's first two governors, Henry Sibley and Alexander Ramsey; Minnesota's first public school teacher, Harriet Bishop; founder of 3M, Archibald Bush; founder of the nation's first hospital for kids with disabilities, Arthur Gillette; heir to the legendary Theodore Hamm Brewing Company, William Hamm; and his famously kidnapped son, William A. Hamm Jr.

But it's also the "people's cemetery" for heroic patriots, early and recent immigrants, and everyday folks who lived extraordinary lives. "Soldiers Rest" in Block 41 is reserved for veterans dating back to the Civil War. Nearby is a towering statue of a fireman carrying a child and lantern, marking the spot reserved for members of the St. Paul Firemen's Association who lost their lives in the line of duty. On the northeast side along Jackson Street is a "county plot" set aside long ago for the Ramsey County poor and former slaves. Some nationalities have their own lots, including Romanians, Chinese, Russians, and Germans. Most recently, it has become a popular burial place for St. Paul's large Hmong community featuring black granite tombstones, etched with portraits and stories.

Each of the 70,000 tombstones at Oakland Cemetery is a symbolic piece of St. Paul's ongoing story. It's a go-to destination for photographers, historians, and genealogists.

Twin Cities Suburbs & Beyond

There are more than 100 suburbs in the Twin Cities. The first-ring suburb of Hopkins—once the nation's raspberry capital—cemented its place in history in April 2022 when its Mainstreet (shown in photo), from Eighth to Eleventh Avenue, was named to the National Register of Historic Places for its significance in American history, architecture, archaeology, engineering, and culture.

Oldest Pro Theater
Old Log Theatre
5185 Meadville St., Greenwood

The vibrant Twin Cities theater scene is a source of local pride, joy, and catharsis. One of its most beloved theatrical gems, nestled on a peaceful 11-acre estate near the shores of Lake Minnetonka, is the Old Log Theatre. Not only is it the oldest professional theater in Minnesota, but it's also often proclaimed the oldest continuously operating professional theater in the US.

It began as a summer theater in 1940 with a new play on stage each week, debuting with *Pennywise*. Admission of 40 cents got you a spot on a hard bench inside a soggy, dirt-floored horse stable, now used as a scenery shop. In the early days, the entire theater crew lived together like a commune in a cobwebby old house across the street owned by a former madam named Emma. Anyone who hadn't learned their lines was given a bucket by other cast members to clean up the cesspool from the overloaded septic system.

During the next two decades, the Old Log established a loyal following and received widespread critical acclaim. In 1960, the current theater complex was built on the property, and the operation became year-round. The exterior resembles a barn while the interior features open beam ceilings, a lobby with a large fireplace, and a fine dining restaurant.

Don Stolz, the theater's longtime owner who died in 2015 at age 97, joined the crew at age 23 as an actor and a director in 1941. But when Pearl Harbor was attacked, he joined the Navy. When he returned in 1946, he purchased the Old Log Summer Repertory group for one dollar from the property owners, the Kuechles. He then leased the property and theater until he could purchase it in the 1960s. Stolz, known as the godfather of the Twin Cities theater community, gave a curtain speech at nearly every show until he sold the venue to Greg and Marissa Frankenfield in 2013.

In addition to contemporary plays and musicals, the Old Log Theatre also produces children's show productions during the summer and holiday seasons. It has been the springboard for many fine performers, including Nick Nolte, Loni Anderson, Lois Nettleton, and Steve Zahn.

OLDEST DUGOUT CANOE
WEST HENNEPIN HISTORY CENTER
1953 West Wayzata Blvd., Long Lake

I n August 1934, during severely low water conditions, brothers Helmer and Arthur Gunnarson were building an extension to the family's dock on the shoreline of Lake Minnetonka's North Arm Bay in Orono. While trying to pound in one of the posts, they hit what they thought was a rock or log.

As they started to dig, they exposed an object deeply embedded in silt and mud. After dragging it out, they determined it was a well-preserved Native American dugout canoe, measuring 11.1 feet long and 1.4 feet wide. These canoes were constructed by hollowing out large tree trunks. They were lifelines to the Indigenous people, who settled near waterways and used them to spear fish and harvest wild rice. During the winter months, they preserved the canoes by burying them in the ground, marking the spot so they could find it again in the spring.

The canoe was donated to the Minnesota Archaeological Society and passed around to various museums. For many years, it was housed at the Minneapolis Public Library. At that time, it was believed to be 200 or 300 years old. In the 1950s, the Western Hennepin County Pioneer Association took the artifact under its wing. A few years later, the association placed the canoe in its museum: the Western Hennepin History Center, a true gem founded in 1907 in the former Long Lake Schoolhouse about six miles from where the canoe was first discovered.

At first, the canoe was placed in the museum's backroom collection of family heirlooms. That is, until Maritime Heritage Minnesota archaeologists Ann Merriman and Chris Olson secured a grant to do a radiocarbon analysis on the canoe and seven other dugout canoes found across the state. Their studies revealed the Lake Minnetonka canoe was constructed from a white oak tree between the years of 1025 and 1165, making it the oldest known watercraft found in the state. This thousand-year treasure is now the museum's centerpiece, enclosed in a glass case.

IF YOU GO: The West Hennepin History Center is free and open to the public on Saturdays 10 a.m.–2 p.m.

Another of these historical dugout canoes can be viewed at Hoċokata Ti, the 3,800-square-foot cultural center of the Shakopee Mdewakanton Sioux community, opened in 2019 in Shakopee.

Courtesy West Hennepin History Center

OLDEST MAGIC SHOP
EAGLE MAGIC STORE
11995 N CR-11, Burnsville

I n this digital age, the sense of awe and wonder surrounding
magic seems to be slowly disappearing. But in the Twin
Cities, there exists a place where reverence for mysteries of
the craft has been preserved for well over a century.

First opened in downtown Minneapolis in 1899, Eagle Magic
claims to be the oldest magic shop in America. At one point,
the shop had multiple locations. Since 2008, the business has
been consolidated into one,
tiny, disheveled shop of
curiosities and wonders
inside a nondescript
commercial building
in suburbia. Much like
the original shop, the
shelves and glass cases are
crammed with antique
pranks along one side
and trickery and illusion
on the other. The back
room is also loaded with
surprises, including a desk
from the 1880s where the
legendary escape artist

*If you have any old magic books or tricks laying
around, longtime shop owner Larry Kahlow
collects those. He's also available for magic shows.*

Harry Houdini once sat while visiting the downtown shop in early years.

The shop's first owner was Collins Pentz, Minnesota's "Dean of Magic." Pentz became interested in magic after seeing Herrmann the Great perform his "Magic, Mirth, and Mystery" show at the Grand Theater in Minneapolis. After Pentz's death in the 1950s, Eagle Magic was taken over by Doris Davids, a longtime employee.

On several occasions, while Doris was sitting in the back room with a couple of her employees, playing cards, eating cheese sandwiches, and drinking Pabst Blue Ribbon in Dixie cups, a 10-year-old boy named Larry Kahlow and his mom would stop in to browse after her hair appointments nearby. Once Larry tried out the whoopie cushions, electric hand buzzers, and cans with fake snakes springing out of them, he was hooked.

By the time Larry was 15, he was performing magic shows at birthday parties. In 1970, he started working at Eagle Magic. By 1976, he owned it. Ever since, he's been working behind the counter while demonstrating tricks to budding magicians. "It's fun to be fooled but more fun to be the fooler," he'll say in his trademark deep voice (if you're lucky).

Since its opening, the Eagle Magic Store has had some famous visitors, including Harry Houdini, David Copperfield, Muhammad Ali, and Steve Martin (who reportedly bought a couple of his trademark arrow-through-the-head props there).

OLDEST MUSIC STORE
GROTH MUSIC
8056 S Nicollet Ave., Bloomington

T he 20,000-square-foot showroom of Groth Music is like a musical candy shop dripping with beautiful things, from crystal flutes and electric egg shakers to bagpipes and conga drums. It also features one of the nation's premier print music departments.

Founded in 1939 by Chester E. Groth, the shop was first located in downtown Minneapolis. In 1985, Chester's daughter, Nancy Groth-Kersten, moved operations to Bloomington inside a former Country Club Market. It's now operated by Chester's

granddaughter, Melanie Peterson, who took flute lessons at the original shop, where Grandpa Chester let her pick out a candy bar before each lesson.

"We know what you want, and we have it," Groth Music claims. And they typically do—except for that one day in 2006, when the Minnesota Vikings called and asked, "Do you guys have a *Gjallarhorn*?" According to

TJ's original Gjallarhorn is now on display at the Minnesota Vikings Museum, adjacent to the practice facility in Eagan, MN. Ccourtesy Minnesota Vikings

Norse mythology, the Gjallarhorn or "hollering horn" was sounded to announce the arrival of the gods.

Groth's staff reached out to their vendors, but nobody seemed to know what a Gjallarhorn was. "Well, then, I'll make one!" said General Manager Todd "TJ" Johnson. It was TJ's initial 10-foot version, made in his garage using fiberglass, PVC pipe, and chicken wire, that launched the tradition of an honorary Viking blowing the Gjallarhorn prior to battles on the gridiron.

A couple of years later, TJ made the team a more refined rendition. However, after the team moved to TCF Bank Stadium while waiting on the new US Bank Stadium, TJ's horn was replaced by a fancier Gjallarhorn custom-made in London. But as fans remember, the poor thing shattered due to frigid temperatures before the January 2016 playoff loss to the Seahawks. Not to worry, though: TJ's reliable, humble horn was rushed in and saved the day.

The story about how the metro's longest-surviving, single brick-and-mortar music store is forever linked to the Minnesota Vikings legacy is a whimsical piece of local history that deserves to be passed along to future generations.

OLDEST SUBURB
RICHFIELD /RICHFIELD HISTORY CENTER
6901 S Lyndale Ave., Richfield

After the hardships and deprivations of World War II, the hallmark of the American Dream became a home in the suburbs. What was once distant farmland flourished into an abundance of affordable subdivisions lined with "crackerbox" tract homes with identical floor plans, matching yards, and nearby Red Owl grocery stores.

Richfield, a first-ring suburb just south of Minneapolis, was the fastest-growing of the Twin Cities suburbs. It also claims to be the state's oldest suburb. That's because its boundaries originally included Camp Coldwater near Fort Snelling, where a trading post drew the first tiny group of non-native settlers and farmers in the 1820s.

Richfield housing development "pushing cows off farm fields, 1954." MNHS Collections

On May 11, 1858, the same day that Minnesota became the 32nd state, a meeting was held to name the township. Richfield was chosen for the fertile farmland that characterized the area. It was incorporated as a village in 1908 and a city in 1960. Through the years, Richfield's boundaries, which originally stretched over 63 square miles, were greatly reduced as it lost jurisdiction over land to neighboring towns, airport expansion, and Fort Snelling.

Today, Richfield's 35,000 residents enjoy a small-town atmosphere within seven square miles, including more than 20 neighborhood and community parks and a strong community spirit. A great place to learn about the suburb's journey is at the Richfield History Center on Lyndale Avenue.

While at the history center, you can tour the Bartholomew House, considered Richfield's oldest private home. It was built long before suburban sprawl by Riley Bartholomew, a general from Ohio's state militia and one of the area's first settlers. After an 1851 treaty with the Dakota opened the area for settlement and Fort Snelling's area was reduced, Bartholomew claimed a piece of land on the east side of Wood Lake to build the home, where he lived with his wife, Fanny, and their four children. Their oldest son, Winfield, later took over the homestead. In 1945, relatives Frank and Agnes Keefe inherited the house and ran the popular Keefe's Farmers Market on the lot until the early 1960s.

Richfield is home to the 150-acre Wood Lake Nature Center, a year-round treasure including an amphitheater, a museum, and two miles of walking trails. A couple of all-terrain wheelchairs are available to reserve.

OLDEST PRIVATE HOME
SIBLEY HISTORIC SITE
1357 Sibley Memorial Hwy., Mendota

Any exploration of Minnesota's early days turns a spotlight on the tiny old village of Mendota (originally named St. Peter's), nestled among bluffs at the confluence of the Minnesota and Mississippi Rivers. First, it was a gathering place for Paleo-Indians thousands of years ago. Later, it was the site for Euro-American fur traders making their way up the river, including Henry Sibley, who became Minnesota's first state governor in 1858.

In 1834, Sibley took over for Alexis Bailly as operations manager for the American Fur Company at Mendota. While there, he lived and worked in a limestone house built on a picturesque site in 1835. Now operated by the Dakota County Historical Society, in partnership with the Minnesota Historical Society, the site is home to four of Minnesota's oldest buildings. The Sibley House is often referred to as the state's oldest private residence.

Sibley lived in the home for 28 years. He first lived there as a bachelor, then with a Dakota woman named Red Blanket Woman and their daughter. In 1843, after their relationship ended, he married Sarah Jane Steele, sister to Franklin Steele. Henry and Sarah Jane had at least nine children, only four of whom survived into adulthood. After they moved to St. Paul in 1862, the house served successively as a convent and industrial school for girls, an art studio, and a place for the homeless. In 1910, it was restored by the Daughters of the American Revolution.

Sibley's role in the US–Dakota War of 1862, and its dark aftermath, including 38 Dakota men hanged in Mankato in the largest mass execution in US history, remains a topic of deeply rooted grief and controversy. Although he was known as a friend to the Dakota while a fur trader, Sibley was appointed by Governor Alexander Ramsey as commander of forces to fight against them. The six-week battle raged through southwestern Minnesota after years of broken treaty promises by the US government. The war's disastrous effects had a profound impact on shaping Minnesota as we know it today.

IF YOU GO: For information about tours, go to www.mnhs.org/sibley.

Follow the road behind Sibley Historic Site to the Sibley Ferry Stone Arch Bridge, the state's oldest railroad bridge (and tunnel) built in 1864. The tracks are now abandoned, but the pathway through the tunnel leads to the Minnesota riverbank.

OLDEST CHURCH IN STATE
HISTORIC CHURCH OF ST. PETER
1405 Hwy. 13, Mendota

With its steeple peeking through trees like a spire reaching toward the heavens, the Historic Church of St. Peter, built in 1853 atop the bluffs on the east bank of the Minnesota River, provides authentic witness to generations of history.

The first dedicated church building for the St. Peter Parish was actually a 20-foot by 40-foot log chapel constructed in 1842 by Father Lucien Galtier of France, the first Catholic priest to serve Minnesota. (He's also the reason our capital city is named St. Paul and not Pig's Eye, but that's a story for another day.) The altar from that log chapel—essentially a rough, three-foot by six-foot cabinet built by Galtier—is still preserved inside the perpetual adoration chapel of the parish's modern church next door, where most church activities are held today. The tabernacle belonging to the historic altar is showcased in the gathering area of the modern church.

When the parish outgrew the 1842 chapel, Galtier's successor, Father Augustine Ravoux, built what's now known as the Historic Church, using stone from a nearby quarry and splitting roof shingles by hand. This charming structure is where Fort Snelling soldiers often attended services. A rectory was added in 1881. Before that, priests lived in the sacristy and the cold attic of the church. On the exterior, it remains much the same as it was back then, except for the steeple, which is the fourth one to adorn the top of the church. One of the steeples came crashing down in a storm. Another was destroyed by a tornado.

Many changes were made to the interior through the years, based on parish needs and each pastor's particular taste. In the mid-1970s, the church closed for extensive renovations. Governed by historical data, the goal was to restore the church to what it would've looked like in about 1890. The renovations cost $284,000, a far cry from the original construction cost of $4,425.

IF YOU GO: The Historic Church is still used for daily Mass, weddings, funerals, and other celebrations. Tours are offered every Sunday, 11 a.m. to 1 p.m., from Memorial Day weekend through mid-September.

Inside, the church's simple beauty is enhanced by silver candlesticks and gold-threaded lace on the altar, antique seating, original wall stencils that had been covered up for many years, and the original organ.

—— AT LEAST 8,000 BCE
OLDEST BLUFFTOP LANDMARK
OȞÉYAWAHE/HISTORIC PILOT KNOB
2044 Pilot Knob Rd., Mendota Heights

Historic Pilot Knob or *Oȟéyawahe*—its Dakota name that translates to "the hill much visited"—offers a spectacular panoramic view of the Mendota Bridge, Fort Snelling, and Twin Cities skylines. But it's also a landmark of Minnesota's beginnings and a Dakota site of great significance and reverence.

After nearly becoming a townhouse development in 2002, the prominent hill was added to the National Register of Historic Places in 2017, citing its ecological, historical, and cultural importance. For centuries, it has been a Native American gathering place and sacred burial ground. It was also where the signing of the 1851 Treaty of Mendota took place, during which the Dakota people ceded 35 million acres to the US government, moving them off their homeland and onto reservations.

Oȟéyawahe/Historic Pilot Knob played an important role in Minnesota's early territorial and state history as well. The "Knob" atop the hill (removed in 1926), was a key reference point for riverboat captains navigating the Minnesota River Valley. Because it was such a distinctive landmark, this site was once considered a potential location for the territorial capital.

A 25-acre portion of the historically preserved 112-acre area, which includes Acacia Cemetery and Park, is owned by

the city of Mendota Heights and stewarded in collaboration with the Pilot Knob Preservation Association. Throughout the past decade, the city's portion has been undergoing restoration. From the parking lot at the north end of Pilot Knob Road, a trail surrounded by wildflowers leads to interpretive signage, scenic overlooks, and the paved Big Rivers Regional Trail below. At one of the overlooks is a sculptural work of art by local artist Seitu Jones—seven blocks of carved stone arranged in a circle as seats for representatives of the seven council fires of the Dakota nation.

IF YOU GO: For directions and more information, visit pilotknobpreservation.org.

Located along the Mississippi Flyway, Oȟéyawahe/ Historic Pilot Knob has extraordinary bird-watching opportunities. Over 325 bird species travel via this migratory route each year.

---1899

OLDEST GRAIN ELEVATOR
PEAVEY-HAGLIN EXPERIMENTAL ELEVATOR
5005 Hwy. 7, St. Louis Park 55416

Whether you're a longtime local or simply love dense fluted cakes with holes in their centers, you probably know that the Bundt pan was invented in Minnesota at the international headquarters for Nordic Ware in St. Louis Park. But you might be surprised to learn the iconic tower overlooking the complex, emblazoned with a Nordic Ware advertisement and their Vikings mascot (named Ole), is a historical landmark that revolutionized the practice of agriculture around the globe.

The tower was actually standing there long before the pioneering kitchenware company came along. Commissioned by Frank Peavey, it was built as an experimental cylindrical concrete grain elevator, the first of its kind in the US and possibly the world. The grain industry has long been a vital part of the Minnesota economy. But in the early days, most grain storage elevators were wooden and at constant risk of catching fire. So Peavey, nicknamed the Elevator King, who owned grain elevators throughout the Midwest, teamed up with Minneapolis contractor Charles Haglin to construct an alternative.

Concrete was selected for its fire resistance and strength while the circular shape was designed to resist internal pressure. Despite plenty of skeptics who thought the concrete would explode or crack, Peavey and Haglin persisted. In May 1899, the tower was successfully filled. The following spring, a crowd gathered to watch as it was emptied, though they kept their distance just in case the naysayers were right. When the grain flowed out without a hitch, everyone cheered.

Although the tower was never used to store grain again, it served as a prototype for all future grain elevators. In 1946, Dave and Dotty Dalquist founded Nordic Ware on the property. In 1996, they invested in a major structural renovation of the tower, earning the right to paint their company logo on it.

IF YOU GO: Look for a new Bundt Café, which was tentatively scheduled to open on the Nordic Ware compound Summer 2023. Also, adjacent to the tower is the Cedar River Trail and Restored Lilac Park (see next story).

In 2012, Artist Randy Walker created a replica of the former grain elevator from steel and lighted ropes to form the "Dream Tower" in front of the nearby Towerlight Senior Living campus.

Oldest Lilac Way Relics
Graeser Park and Restored Lilac Park
Robbinsdale and St. Louis Park

I t's hard to imagine now, but driving along Highway 100 was
once a leisurely, parkway-like experience. When the west-
metro thoroughfare was first laid out, the 12.5-mile showcase
section between Edina and Robbinsdale, coined Lilac Way, was
considered one of America's most scenic drives.

Created during the Great
Depression, the goal was
to beautify the highway
while creating as many jobs
as possible. The result? A
corridor peppered with
thousands of lilac bushes
and seven roadside parks
designed by Arthur Nichols,
accentuated by ornamental
ponds, rock gardens, stone
picnic tables, and 10-foot-tall,
beehive-shaped fireplaces used for grilling.

Graeser Park, Robbinsdale

This extraordinary endeavor was the brainchild of Carl
Graeser, an engineer for the Minnesota Highway Department
(now MnDOT). In collaboration with the WPA, Graeser gave
nearly 4,000 homeless men 40 hours of employment each
month for 55 cents an hour to complete the project.

Lost in the late 1990s: Lilac Park (original, Mtka. Blvd).
Courtesy MnDOT

Only two of the parks remain. One is Graeser Park in Robbinsdale at West Broadway and Lakeland Avenues. As part of ongoing updates, MnDOT recently restored Graeser Park's remaining beehive fireplace and rebuilt 11 stone tables using salvaged stone from Graeser and other lost Lilac Way Parks. The other is Restored Lilac Park at Highways 100 and 7. That park features a 100-foot wall of lilacs blooming in May, five limestone picnic tables, signage detailing the history, and a beehive fireplace relocated from the original Lilac Park that was north of Minnetonka Boulevard.

Remains of that original Lilac Park, razed due to road construction, can be seen tucked behind a 20-foot sound barrier on the west side of Toledo Avenue on the 2800 block. The fate of that parcel of history, now referred to as Rock Island Park, was still under discussion as this book went to press. Check www.restorelilacway.com for photos and updates.

Only two beehive fireplaces remain in the US, and those are located at Graeser Park and Restored Lilac Park. Graeser's is the only one in its original location.

Oldest Public Wildflower Garden
Eloise Butler Wildflower Garden
1 Theodore Wirth Pkwy., Golden Valley

Nestled within Theodore Wirth Park, close enough to downtown Minneapolis to see the IDS Center glowing at night, is a hidden oasis—the Eloise Butler Wildflower Garden and Bird Sanctuary. It's tucked behind a beautiful gated entrance inscribed with the words "Let Nature Be Your Teacher."

Dating back to 1907, this 15-acre treasure is the oldest public wildflower garden in North America. In 1874, at age 23, Eloise Butler moved from Maine to Minneapolis to teach school. Passionate about connecting young people with nature, she'd take her students on hikes in search of rare native flora. A 1906 South High School yearbook warns against taking classes with Butler "unless you enjoy 10-mile walks through bog and swamp."

With concerns about the growing city of Minneapolis encroaching on natural areas, Butler and three other botany teachers wanted to create a natural botanic garden. In 1907, they successfully petitioned the park board to set aside a small portion of Glenwood Park, which was later renamed after Minneapolis Parks Superintendent Theodore Wirth. As the garden's first curator, Butler shaped the grounds for 26 years with an unwavering spirit. On April 10, 1933, at age 81, she died

LET NATURE BE YOUR TEACHER

of a heart attack on her way to tend the garden. Her ashes were scattered among her wildflowers.

The garden now harbors more than 500 native plant varieties and 130 migratory bird species. Visitors follow a winding, one-mile trail, cushioned with wood chips and dotted with interpretive stations. Running through three different ecosystems, the trail takes you deep into a natural green world beneath a canopy of trees, across a burbling creek, and past grassy fields.

IF YOU GO: The garden is open and free to the public April 1 to October 15, Tuesday through Sunday, from 7:30 a.m. to 6 p.m. Bring mosquito spray!

After visiting the historic garden, check out the nearby Quaking Bog, a short hike through a five-acre wetland area. It features a floating boardwalk through a rare and delicate ecosystem of mosses and tamaracks.

Oldest Bar in State

Neumann's Bar

2531 E 7th Ave., North St. Paul

Where can you drink icy cold Hamm's beer in the company of frogs named Betty Croaker and Dennis Hopper? That'll be Neumann's in North St. Paul, which claims to be the oldest continuously operating bar in Minnesota, in part because it's the oldest one still around that kept serving booze during Prohibition.

Neumann's began as a workingman's bar. Today, it's a charming neighborhood spot that appeals to everyone from bikers to business folks. Its rugged floors, tin ceilings, mahogany bar, silver cash register, and mounted animal heads are the same as they were in the days when patrons in suspenders and cowboy chaps played cards at the back tables.

Hamm's Brewing Company struck a deal with Bill Neumann to open the bar in 1887. Back then, it was common for beer manufacturers to provide space in exchange for exclusively selling

their beer. Before the bar was purchased by a local customer, it was owned by three generations of the Neumann family.

When the sale of alcohol in the US was banned in the 1920s, Neumann's survived by selling fish bait out of the basement, near-beer from the main floor, and illegal hooch from the second floor that's now mostly used for special events. If you climb the staircase hidden behind a door by the frog tank, you'll see the peephole they used to size people up. You'll also see an old crank phone that used to be connected to another telephone behind the main floor bar, which bartenders used to alert one another when cops came sniffing around.

Author's Note: The Spot Bar in St. Paul's West Seventh neighborhood also claims to be Minnesota's longest continuously running bar. Read about that rustic gem in my 2020 book, *Secret Twin Cities: A Guide to the Weird, Wonderful, and Obscure.*

To the best of anyone's memory, the tank of frogs in the front window has been a trademark tradition at Neumann's since around 1930. The frogs have occasionally gone missing. One of them was once found in a pitcher of beer!

OLDEST SKATE SHOP
STRAUSS SKATES AND BICYCLES
1751 E Cope Ave., Maplewood

There's just something about the sound of blades echoing across a sheet of ice that brings us Minnesotans joy. And if you've lived here for a while, there's a good chance you've had a pair of skates made or sharpened by the Strauss family, founders of Strauss Skate Shop, which claims to be the oldest skate shop in the country and quite possibly in the world.

After immigrating to the US from Germany in the early 1880s, John Strauss Sr. worked at his brother Emil's locksmith shop in Chicago. In 1887, he moved to St. Paul and opened his own shop, originally located where the downtown Xcel Energy Center now stands. When he tired of cutting keys, he incorporated a bike business. Since many of his bike racing customers skated in the winter to stay in shape, they encouraged him to apply his metalworking skills to make and repair ice skates.

Strauss created the first closed-toe blade using a secret

Original Downtown Shop. Courtesy Strauss Skate Shop

hardening process that he had learned while working in an arsenal in Italy. Made from high-carbon steel, the Strauss blades were lighter and stronger for jumping and spinning. Strauss made his first pair of figure skates in 1888 for local athlete Harley Davidson. The next year, he made his first pair of racing skates for Axel Paulsen, inventor of the "axel" skating jump. He added

Sonja Henie won Olympic Gold on Strauss blades in 1928. Courtesy Strauss Skate Shop

hockey skates to his repertoire a few years later.

In 1941, Strauss's son, John Jr., bought the business. Four decades later, John Jr.'s nephew, Donald, took over with longtime partners Richard and Liz Charbonneau. Since Donald's passing in 2015, the Charbonneau family has carried on the legacy, which now operates from a big, old, yellow-brick building in Maplewood, 15 minutes northeast of downtown St. Paul.

Strauss skates were made by hand at Strauss Skate Shop for nearly a hundred years. In 1980, John Jr. made the last pair of skates by hand, using the revolutionary technique his father had developed.

OLDEST LUTHERAN CHURCH
GAMMELKYRKAN AT GAMMELGÅRDEN MUSEUM
20796 Olinda Trl., Scandia

Outside of Sweden, Minnesota has more people with Swedish ancestry than any other place in the world. Encouraged by the state's fertile farmland, they came by the thousands starting in the 1850s. It's believed that the first Swedish immigrants settled in Scandia, a small town on the northeast edge of the Twin Cities, where vibrantly colorful Swedish Dala horse statues welcome visitors.

Just past the city center is the lush, 11-acre, open-air Gammelgården Museum. More like a farm, the museum tells the story of early Swedish immigration through a collection of five historic furnished buildings. One of them is a log sanctuary known as the Gammelkyrkan. The museum claims this 20-foot by 30-foot treasure, constructed in 1856, is Minnesota's oldest Lutheran church building.

Originally located two miles south of the museum, it served as the first church for the Elim Lutheran congregation, which is now housed in a much larger structure across from North Elim Lutheran Cemetery. Throughout its long history, Elim has been through a tornado and two fires that razed its buildings to the ground each time.

By 1860, the congregation had already outgrown the little sanctuary. As a result, it was moved and used to house Hay Lake School until 1899. Then it was sold, dismantled, and moved to the Frank Forsell farm. The Forsell family later donated it to the Gammelgården Museum, which opened in 1972. Sunday morning church services are still held in the historic structure from Memorial Day through Labor Day.

The museum offers guided tours and special events, which include traditional Swedish celebrations, Mid-Sommar Dag, Fiddling Fest, and interactive activities such as making butter, crafting hand-carved wooden toys, and playing old-fashioned games. For Nordic-inspired treats, gifts, and souvenirs, check out the gift shop (Butik), located in the main building (Välkommen Hus).

IF YOU GO: The museum and gift shop are open May through mid-October with guided tours (free for children under age 12) every Friday, Saturday, and Sunday at 1:30 p.m.

Scandia is part of the Washington County Barn Quilt Trail, a beautiful and historical 16-mile route that winds along the St. Croix River. Along the way are 18 barns with quilt-patterned roofs based on patterns from the book The Quiltmaker's Gift.

1849
OLDEST GENERAL STORE
MARINE GENERAL STORE
101 Judd St., Marine on St. Croix

I f you're looking to get away from big-city energy, Marine on St. Croix is a wonderful choice. Located about 30 miles northeast of St. Paul and 15 miles south of Taylors Falls, the quaint town feels like you've stepped into a 19th-century New England village.

While there, if you need anything—anything at all—from camping gear, onion choppers, and beach shoes to dry goods, goat milk, or a peach pie, you'll likely find it at the Marine General Store, which still has the original counters and creaky floors from its pre-Civil War days. It's the town's centerpiece and the oldest continually operating general store in Minnesota.

The store was first built in 1849 a few doors down and named Marine Lumber Company, which sold "a little of most everything." After that structure burned down in 1867, a new store was built at the current site. Although the landmark emporium has had a long line of owners, Ralph Malmberg, who owned it in the 1960s, is probably the most acclaimed—thanks to frequent customer Garrison Keillor. In Keillor's legendary *News from Lake Wobegon* radio show, he often mentioned "Ralph's Pretty Good Grocery Store." He'd say, "If you can't find it at Ralph's, you can probably get along without it," a motto he openly admits he stole from his landlady.

On the backside of the store, where the store's chicken coop used to be, there's an ice cream shop with a big pink ice cream cone painted on the outside wall. A fixture in downtown Marine on St. Croix since 1977, Nita Mae's Scoop (as it's now called), moved to this spot in 1999. There's also a bait shop back there and a trail that leads down to the St. Croix River.

IF YOU GO: Down the road from the General Store is the Marine Mill site, spotlighting the remnants and ruins of Minnesota's first commercial sawmill. Built in 1839, the mill operated for nearly six decades. Overlooks and pathways with interpretive signs provide visitors with a glimpse of the industry that helped build Minnesota.

Two miles north of the general store is William O'Brien State Park. A stone's throw from the park is Crabtree's Garden Gate, a must-see for anyone into whimsical outdoor garden art.

OLDEST COURTHOUSE
WASHINGTON COUNTY HISTORIC COURTHOUSE
101 W Pine St., Stillwater

Minnesota's longest-standing courthouse, which served Washington County until 1975, is an architectural treasure overlooking the St. Croix River Valley. Now a museum with history-based activities and tours, it's a fascinating place to soak up the backstories of the people who worked and got locked up behind bars there.

After the previous three-room courthouse became too cramped, the city purchased this property on Zion's Hill to build a new one, completed in 1870. Construction slowed when the scaffolding collapsed in 1868, throwing workers to the ground. One of the bricklayers from Minneapolis died after somersaulting some 50 feet in the air and landing on his head. The Italianate and Greek Revival structure, designed by Augusta F. Knight, features an imposing dome, cupola and flagpole, 11 brick chimneys rising from the roof, the courthouse, a jailhouse, and sheriff's residence.

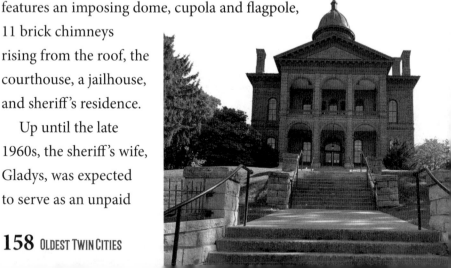

Up until the late 1960s, the sheriff's wife, Gladys, was expected to serve as an unpaid cook and laundress. Its most famous prisoners were the three Younger brothers—Cole, Bob, and Jim—of the notorious Jesse James Gang. The original jail was a two-story structure with four cells on each floor. In 1900, a 12-cell jail was added, which is available during public and self-guided tours. Look for graffiti left by inmates on the walls and ceilings. The original jail cells are available only during the Nooks & Crannies tours.

Thanks to a spirited campaign by concerned citizens, the historic judicial center was saved from demolition in the 1960s after it became inadequate for its initial purpose. As you enter the main doors, you'll walk into a large central hallway with arched entryways, iron doors, and multicolored ceramic floors. A grand double staircase ascends to the large courtroom. During the Nooks & Crannies tour, you'll climb another staircase to the attic, then another spiraling staircase to the dome for breathtaking views.

IF YOU GO: Admission is free. Donations are accepted. Check www.co.washington.mn.us/hc for more information about public tours, neighborhood history strolls, and special tours that explore areas of the courthouse that are typically closed off to the public.

To the northeast of the courthouse stands the Soldiers & Sailors Civil War Monument, dedicated to the Minnesota Volunteer Infantry Regiment. Down the staircase and across the street stands the Stillwater Veterans Memorial in the shape of a church steeple, honoring students of Stillwater Area Schools who lost their lives in military service to their country

---

Oldest Ice Cream Shop
Selma's Ice Cream Parlor
3419 St. Croix Trail S, Afton

Nothing takes you back to simpler times like an ice cream parlor tucked inside a red-and-white cottage decorated in gingerbread trim. Located in Afton, a rural river town about 15 miles east of downtown St. Paul, Selma's fits the bill as Minnesota's oldest operating ice cream parlor. It's a wonderful little place to grab a taste of old-fashioned sweetness.

Upon entering, take in a whiff of home-baked waffle cones while feasting your eyes on corner shelves loaded with licorice ropes and lollipops. Then, it's time to treat yourself to two scoops of award-winning ice cream with endearing names like Yippee Skippie, Exhausted Parent, Heaps of Love, and This $&@! Just Got Serious.

The original structure was built as a private home in 1880 by the Holberg family. A few decades later, family descendant Eddie Holberg and his wife, Selma, converted their living room into a confectionery shop with a piano. After Eddie passed away, Selma continued to build the business for another 30 years. An astute businesswoman, Selma also operated a cafe, beer tavern, and small casino on site. Over the years, a structure attached to the north side served as a grocery store, bait shop, and post office.

In 1965, the shop was almost entirely submerged when a record-breaking flood hit the town. Thanks to fellow Afton resident and business owner Elmer H. Smith, who offered to pay to fix the damages, the store was saved. Selma served ice cream until the day she died in 1966. Since then, owners have come and gone. "I never had a bad day at Selma's," said Kelly McGee (*Star Tribune*, 2011), who managed the shop when her mother, Laine, owned it from 1981 to 2007.

In 2009, ice cream lovers mourned as the shop went into foreclosure and was shuttered. In 2012, Paul and Becky Nickerson, committed to continuing the legacy, reopened it. With six children, the Nickersons had a built-in crew to wipe counters, make waffle cones, serve malts and floats, and help carry on this landmark piece of Americana.

Four miles south from the ice cream shop is Afton State Park with trails and bluffs overlooking the St. Croix River, a swimming beach, and visitor center with interpretive displays.

Oldest Winery
Alexis Bailly Vineyard
18200 S Kirby Ave., Hastings

We all know surviving a Minnesota winter involves some suffering. But try being a grape. According to French winemakers, though, it's good for grapevines to suffer through a little wind, sleet, and snow. In 1973, David Bailly, a Minneapolis attorney and fine wine connoisseur, set out to prove that theory true. He purchased a 20-acre field on the edge of Hastings, 30 minutes southeast of St. Paul, and planted Minnesota's first vineyard in one of the world's most difficult climates.

To survive the frigid temperatures, each vine had to be laid down and covered with dirt in autumn. Meanwhile, Bailly constructed a cozy winery of Minnesota limestone and white knotty pine. He named it after his ancestor, Alexis Bailly, a French fur trader and one of the founders of Hastings in the

1800s. Look for framed photos of Bailly and of David hanging in the rustic, twinkly-lit tasting room.

In 1978, Alexis Bailly Vineyard, "where the grapes suffer," made history when it released the first wines ever produced commercially with 100 percent Minnesota-grown grapes. Alexis Bailly wines have won more than 45 national awards and can be found at nearly every liquor store in the Twin Cities and on the menu of numerous restaurants.

Tucked away off a gravel road, the vineyard is a lovely spot to catch a slice of Sonoma. Walk through the grounds, purchase local cheeses and salami from the gift shop, and sip a glass of Ratafia or Chocolate Reserve on the trellised patio. In the winter, enjoy warm mulled wine next to outdoor fire pits or reserve a heated outdoor wine yurt. Today, David Bailly's daughter, Nan Bailly, continues the family tradition as owner, winegrower, and master winemaker. She honed her winemaking experience through apprenticeships and stints in upstate New York and France.

IF YOU GO: Open year-round, Fridays, Saturdays, and Sundays from noon to 5 p.m. Join the Alexis Bailly Vineyard Wine Club for a complimentary tasting.

Hastings is also home to the Black Dirt Theater, a group of passionate folks performing original works, from live improv to radio theater, at the Hastings Arts Center.

OLDEST HOTEL
HISTORIC ANDERSON HOUSE
333 W Main St., Wabasha

Nestled among limestone bluffs, 70 miles southeast of the Twin Cities, Wabasha is a quiet river town with an abundance of history, attractions, and eagles. Some may know it best as the setting for the 1990s iconic film *Grumpy Old Men*.

More than 50 buildings in this small town are listed in the National Register of Historic Places, including the Historic Anderson House, Minnesota's oldest hotel, operating since 1856. One block from the Mississippi River, this gem features 22 antique-filled rooms, wraparound gardens, a carriage-house rental, sauna, patio, and sun porch, as well as a new bakery and coffee shop.

First known as the Hurd House, the hotel was renamed when William Anderson and his wife, Ida, purchased it in 1909. In its glory days, the Anderson House drew people from all over the country for Ida's legendary meals cooked up in her Dutch kitchen and served in the cozy dining room. Some may remember the hotel's famed collection of cats, which guests could rent to help "purr" them to sleep. Not surprisingly, the place is said to be haunted by the spirit of a long-ago guest, named Sarah, found lying dead in the hallway. Cause of death was "old age," according to the hotel's operations manager, although many other versions of the story have circulated.

After William and Ida retired, their offspring continued the family legacy. They even published a few cookbooks commemorating "Mother Anderson's" Dutch recipes. In 2001, the hotel was sold outside of the family to Brian and Rachel Yenter. Then, in 2020, Grant Carlson purchased the venue with a group of investors who are now operating it as a hotel and short-term vacation rental.

The cats are gone, Ida's old dining room is now a game room, and contact services have been pared down. But it's still a lovely getaway with complimentary coffee, tea, and oatmeal available in the parlor. Carlson hopes to reopen the Lost Dutchman, a speakeasy-style bar formerly in the basement. He's also working with Twin Cities area chefs on a rotating schedule to provide a variety of meals prepared pop-up style.

The Anderson House is a quiet respite after visiting the National Eagle Center or walking along the river and perusing art galleries. If you're in the area with young kids, drive 10 minutes south to LARK Toys, the coolest toy store, where you can ride on a carousel that was handmade from Minnesota wood.

OLDEST COVERED BRIDGE
ZUMBROTA COVERED BRIDGE
175 West Ave., Zumbrota

F eatured in novels and Hollywood's fleeting-love stories, covered bridges are enduring reminders of America's rural, rustic past. Nearly 12,000 authentic, covered, timber-truss bridges, mostly built throughout the 1800s, once existed in the US. But due to arson, floods, and neglect, only 850 are still standing according to the National Society for the Preservation of Covered Bridges.

Minnesota is home to one of those original timbered treasures. It's a charming, barn-red, 123-foot structure adorned with crisscrossing white pine timbers. It crosses the Zumbro River within Covered Bridge Park, located 60 miles south of the Twin Cities in the quintessential small town of Zumbrota.

Built in 1869, the Zumbrota Covered Bridge, as it's aptly called, was originally a river crossing for stagecoaches and horseback riders. Now the town's pride and joy, it connects parts of the Goodhue Pioneer Regional Trail and serves as a river crossing for pedestrians and bikers on their way to the public swimming pool or downtown Zumbrota.

The bridge was first constructed without a roof. The roof was added in 1871 to protect the bridge deck and trusses from decay. In 1932, the state's Department of Transportation replaced the covered bridge with a steel bridge that could handle increased automobile traffic. The covered bridge was then moved to the Goodhue County Fairgrounds, where it remained for 37 years. There, it housed poultry and wildlife exhibits and later served as a beer hall, earning the title of "the Longest Bar in Goodhue County." In 1965, the bridge was moved to the south side of the Zumbro River before it was relocated to its current location in 1970.

Just before the town was to celebrate the bridge's 150th birthday in 2019, the roof sank under the weight of heavy snow. To replace the bridge without compromising its place in the National Register of Historic Places, construction crews were paid $300,000 to repair it following the original blueprints and using 1860s building materials and techniques.

Plan for your visit to the bridge to include a hike along the Goodhue Pioneer Regional Trail, tucked within Covered Bridge Park. The trail passes through a varied mix of terrain between Goodhue and Red Wing.

OLDEST OBSERVATORY
GOODSELL OBSERVATORY
Carleton College, Northfield

Whether you're into astronomy or not, viewing stars, planets, and the moon through a magnificent telescope built in the late 19th century would be a pretty cool family outing or date night. On the first Friday of

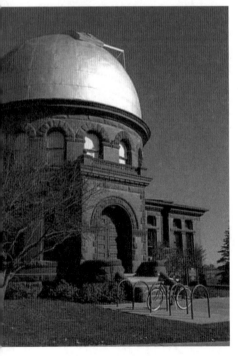

Courtesy Carleton College

each month, you can do exactly that by driving 30 minutes south of the Twin Cities to Carleton College in Northfield. That's when the campus's historic and architecturally beautiful Goodsell Observatory opens to the public, unless it's cloudy.

As the oldest observatory in Minnesota, Goodsell has played a significant role in America's history of astronomy. Among the many accomplishments associated with the observatory, it's where the preeminent astrophysics journal *Astronomy & Astrophysics* was born and where the first Minnesota state weather systems were founded. The observatory is named after the college's founder, Charles M. Goodsell. But it was Professor William Wallace Payne who put this rural Minnesota college on the celestial map.

During Payne's first year teaching on campus, he lobbied for Carleton's first observatory. It was a small, wooden structure completed in 1878 on the grounds where Laird Hall now stands. In 1885, Payne lobbied for the college to build a bigger and better one, and construction of Goodsell Observatory began.

Goodsell has been more than a hub for astronomy, though. The observatory also became a center for timekeeping for the railroad industry. Timekeeping is what keeps trains from colliding, of course, and Goodsell Observatory was equipped with the most sophisticated clocks of the day. After all, timekeeping was one of the first efforts performed by astronomers. They determined the time by measuring the location of celestial bodies. Payne, a true visionary, installed a telegraph line at the observatory and started a time service. Before long, it was the time stamp for all major railroads from Chicago to Seattle. Its signal was considered the most accurate for railroads west of the Mississippi.

IF YOU GO: If there is any doubt about evening viewing conditions, the final decision will be posted an hour or two prior to an Open House at www.carleton.edu/goodsell.

The Goodsell Observatory is also home to one of the most complete college collections of meteorites. Most of the extraterrestrial rocks came from Dr. Harvey H. Nininger, who donated them in lieu of his daughter's tuition.

OLDEST WOOL MILL
FARIBAULT MILL
1500 NW 2nd Ave., Faribault

A long the quiet waters of the Cannon River, about an hour south of the Twin Cities, there's an unassuming, red-brick building filled with century-old machinery and the loud whirring of electric looms. It's the longtime home of Faribault Mill, one of the last vertical woolen mills in America where all phases of production are entirely contained in one site.

Founded the year Lincoln died and the Civil War ended, the mill has provided surprisingly soft wool blankets for pioneers sleeping under the stars, troops shivering in barracks during two world wars, and Team USA snuggling up between Olympic games.

The legacy began when German cabinetmaker Carl Henry Klemer read an editorial about an increase in sheep flocks. As a result, he decided to invest in a carding machine, powered by his horse named Jenny. Still the heart of any wool mill today, a carding machine works like a mechanical brush as it combs out impurities from clumps of raw wool. From the resulting wool strands, Klemer made batting to sell for stuffing quilts or spinning into yarn. Before long, he added yarn-making to his own arsenal of skills, then began churning out blankets. Today, the product line also includes mittens, shawls, caps, pillowcases, baby blankets, and more.

The mill first opened in 1865 inside a stone building along the nearby Straight River. That building was devastated by fire

in 1892. Two years later, a new fireproof brick structure was built at the current location, now listed in the National Register of Historic Places. The Klemers continued to manage the mill for generations. By 1977, the mill was producing half of the blankets made in America. In 2009, due to the recession, it closed, and the equipment was tagged for sale to be shipped overseas. But fortunately, in 2011, cousins Chuck and Paul Mooty reopened and even expanded the mill while bringing back many former workers.

IF YOU GO: Tours are offered every Friday and Saturday at 11 a.m. and 1:00 p.m., at a cost of $5–$10. Call for reservations: 507-412-5534.

The mill is adjacent to the Rice County Fairgrounds and Rice County Museum, where you can learn about the region through artifacts, images, and a 12-minute slide show.

Oldest
Continuous Brewery
August Schell Brewing Company
1860 Schell's Rd., New Ulm

O ften proclaimed "the most German town in America," New Ulm is a city of charm and tradition, located 90 miles southwest of the Twin Cities. One of its most treasured German influences is the August Schell Brewing Company. It's nestled on a river bluff with a canopy of giant black walnut trees opening to beautiful old brick buildings, a fairytale-like mansion, beer garden, and deer park with roaming peacocks.

A family-owned business since 1860, Schell's is the oldest brewery in Minnesota and the second oldest continuously family-owned brewery in the US. It also became the largest brewery in Minnesota when the company bought the rights to Grain Belt in 2002. They're the reason the neon lights glowing from the iconic Grain Belt bottle cap sign on Nicollet Island in Minneapolis got flipped back on in 2017 after going dark for 14 years.

The brewery's rich history begins with August Schell. Born in Durbach, Germany, he left his homeland for the US at age 20. After working as a machinist in Cincinnati, he settled in Minnesota with his wife, Theresa, and their two daughters. Longing for a good German beer, he partnered with brewmaster Jacob Bernhardt to open a brewery along the banks of the Cottonwood River. In that location, they were vulnerable targets during the US–Dakota War of 1862 that nearly destroyed the surrounding area. The Schells, however, had established themselves as friends to the Dakota people, so the brewery was spared.

When August died in 1891, Theresa and the youngest Schell son, Otto, took the reins. When Otto died in 1911, August's brother-in-law, George Marti, successfully shepherded the business through Prohibition, shifting to production of near beer, soft drinks, and candy. The Marti side of the family has kept the old-world legacy alive and flourishing ever since.

IF YOU GO: The brewery's 60-minute, first-come, first-served weekend tours, including sampling, are well worth the $10 price of admission.

Courtesy Schell Brewing Company

While in New Ulm, climb the staircase to the top of the 102-foot Hermann the German monument at Hermann Heights Park for a panoramic view.

OLDEST SAVU SAUNA
FINNISH PIONEER PARK
100 SW Cty Rd. 3, Cokato

In native Finnish culture, a sauna is nearly a holy place. Finns have been sweating head to toe while relaxing, meditating, bathing, socializing, giving birth, and preparing smoked fish in the suffusing glow of those dimly lit, log-paneled rooms for centuries. It's a tradition they bring wherever they go, even to the rural Minnesota town of Cokato. Located about an hour west of Minneapolis, Cokato is home to the oldest Finnish Savu Sauna in North America.

Finns first came to Minnesota in 1864. Although Cokato wasn't the first place they settled, many gravitated there because of its available farmland. In 1868, three of the local Finnish families—the Barbergs, Selvalas, and Salmonsons—pooled resources to build Minnesota's first Savu Sauna on the Wright County line. A Savu Sauna is the oldest type of Finnish sauna: "An open fire would heat the stones, and all smoke exited through vents in the log walls before the fire died out and bathing commenced" (*The Opposite of Cold*, 2010).

After a week of exhausting labor, the early Finnish settlers went to their sauna to relax, sweat off the grime, and socialize. Then, they'd quickly cool off and put their clothes back on in the open air. Well, you can imagine the speculation that this strange, "risqué" tradition began to stir within the non-Finn community, especially when a county road was constructed alongside it. Rumors ran amuck and eventually landed them all in court.

Ultimately, the three families proved they were upstanding citizens and good Lutherans. They even won $30 in damages. But they were still ordered to relocate their sauna to a more private location. In 1976, it was donated to the Cokato Finnish-American Historical Society and moved to Temperance Corner at Finnish Pioneer Park, three miles outside of Cokato. The park features a group of 19th-century buildings that celebrate Finland's cultural heritage through tours and events. Although the sauna no longer functions as a sauna, it has been fully restored to its original 1868 appearance.

Another potential site to add to your day trip to Cokato is Minnesota Pioneer Park located 16 miles north of Cokato in Annandale, spotlighting artifacts and buildings that portray Central Minnesota's pioneer heritage from the late 1800s and early 1900s.

Courtesy Cokato Finnish-American Historical Society

SOURCES

Oldest Family Steakhouse: Site visit Oct. 2, 2022; Phone interview with Bill Kozlak Aug. 24, 2022; www.jaxcafe.com; "Restaurants: Jax Cafe: 75 Birthday Candles." *Star Tribune.* April 9, 2008; "For More Than 50 Years, Jax Café Creates Personal, Embossed Matchbooks for Guests." CBS Minnesota News. Feb. 28, 2019

Oldest Northside Theater: Email correspondence with Janet Zahn; "Landmarks: Paradise Theater." *Minnesota History Magazine.* Summer 2020. p.53; "$12.5 Million Capri Theater Renovation Pinned as Linchpin to North Minneapolis Revitalization. *Star Tribune.* Oct. 22, 2019; "The Renovated Capri Theater Remains a Cultural Hub of North Minneapolis." *Star Tribune.* Sept. 15, 2022; https://princesongs.org/2017/02/08/i-am-you-capri-theatre-january-5-6-1979; https://www.thecurrent.org/feature/2014/01/10/then-and-now-the-capri-theater-where-prince-played-his-first-solo-show; https://becoming.prince.com/story/; https://thecapri.org/; http://digitours.augsburg.edu

Oldest Neighborhood (Minneapolis): Many site visits; Email correspondence with Penny Petersen; www.marcy-holmes.org; "Intro - Hiding in Plain Sight History Tour." *Minneapolis Historical;* "6th Ave. Gateway Sculptures." *Minneapolis Historical;* Learn more by reading *Hiding in Plain Sight: Minneapolis' First Neighborhood* by Penny Petersen, Marcy-Holmes Neighborhood Association

Oldest Street: Many site visits; Email correspondence with Penny Petersen; Penny Petersen. *Hiding in Plain Sight: Minneapolis' First Neighborhood.* pp. 122; "Main Street Buildings (1855, 1858 and 1890)." *Minnesota Historical;* "Main Street Full of History." *Northeaster Newspaper.* Aug. 26, 2021; "From the Strib's Archives: Pracna on Main." *Star Tribune.* Jan. 8, 2015; "Streetscapes: Pracna on Main Defined the Changing Riverfront."*Star Tribune.* April 6, 2015

Oldest Continuous Church: Site visit June 30, 2022; Email correspondence with Mary Asp and review by longtime volunteer parishioners; https://lourdesmpls.org/; http://www.placeography.org; Larry Millet. *AIA Guide to the Twin Cities: The Essential Source on the Architecture of Minneapolis and St. Paul.* MNHS Press; Penny Petersen. *Hiding in Plain Sight: Minneapolis' First Neighborhood.* pp. 30–32.

Oldest Frame House: Site visit Summer 2019; "The Oldest House in the City." *Mill City Times.* June 4, 2021; http://www.womansclub.org/; "Ard Godfrey House, Chute Square." Minneapolis Riverfront Partnership. *Minneapolis Historical;* https://www.minneapolisparks.org/; Penny Petersen. *Hiding in Plain Sight: Minneapolis' First Neighborhood.* pp. 44–45

Oldest Island Venue: Site visit Sept. 21, 2022. "1893 Nicollet Island Northeast Fire." *Mill City Times.* April 12, 2021; https://www.nicolletislandinn.com/about/our-story/; https://charamana.com/2021/09/28/nicollet/; https://www.mnhs.org/places/safhb/final_report.pdf

Oldest Train Hub: Self-Guided Tour April 26, 2021; Email correspondence with Robert Payne; "The Depot in Minneapolis is Closing in on Its Latest Transformation." *Star Tribune.* Oct. 11, 2018; "Milwaukee Depot." Submitted by Preserve Minneapolis. *Minneapolis Historical;* www.placeography.org; www.thedepotminneapolis.com/history/; www.marriott.com/hotels/travel/mspdd-renaissance-minneapolis-hotel-the-depot

Oldest Flour Mill Site: Email correspondences with Molly Jessup and Bill Convery; Numerous site visits; Iric Nathanson. "Washburn A Mill Explosion, 1878." *MNopedia,* MNHS; www.mnhs.org/millcity/learn/history/building; www.mvp.usace.army.mil/Media/News-Stories/Article/626089/engineering-the-falls-the-corps-of-engineers-role-at-st-anthony-falls/; www.goldmedalflour.com/our-story/

Oldest Bridge Relics: Email correspondence with Robin Smothers; Numerous site visits; Matt Reicher. "Father Louis Hennepin Suspension Bridge." *MNopedia,* MNHS; www.nps.gov/miss/planyourvisit/firstbridge

Oldest Northloop Bar: Site visit June 6, 2022; "As Popular as it was 100 Years Ago:The North Loop." *The Journal.* Aug. 31, 2016; "Best Bars with History in Minnesota." *CBS Minnesota.* Oct. 24, 2013; "Landmark North Loop Restaurant Monte Carlo Reopens After First Closure in 100 Plus Years." *Star Tribune.* Aug. 07, 2020; "Monte Carlo's Longevity Due to More Than Just Great Wings."*CBS Minnesota.* Jan. 11, 2018; https://northloop.org/directory/business/the-monte-carlo/; https://discoverthecities.com/north-loop-neighborhood-minneapolis

Oldest Skyscraper: Site visit May 3, 2022; Email correspondence with Barb Culbertson and Pat Hughes; Larry Millett. 2007. *AIA Guide to the Twin Cities: The Essential Source on the Architecture of Minneapolis and St. Paul.* pp. 42–43. MNHS Press; "Minneapolis, The World's Greatest Lumber Center." *Minneapolis Journal,* Nov. 26, 1903—Silver Anniversary Edition; https://www.lileks.com/mpls/lumber/index.html; Wermiel, Sara. "The Minneapolis Lumber Exchange Fire of 1891 and Fire Resisting Construction." *Minnesota History,* 2014, pp 119-128; "The Lumber Exchange Building." Submitted by Preserve Minneapolis. *Minneapolis Historical*

Oldest Downtown Bar: Site visit with Kaz Treharne May 3, 2022; "Three Generations of Brewers in Gluek Family," *Minneapolis Tribune*, July 20, 1936. Star Tribune Archive; https://hennepinhistory.org/older-than-minnesota-gluek-brewing/; "A Long Time A-Brewing." *My Northeaster.* Sept. 17, 2018; "After 153 years, It's Last Call for Gluek Beer "*Star Tribune.* Aug. 4, 2010; Gluek Beer Returns After 160 Years." BeerConnoisseur.com. June 7, 2017; "A 160-Year-Old Minnesota Beer Is Coming Back to Life on Friday." Star Tribune. May 25, 2017; www.glueks.com; https://www.mnbeer.com/history/; https://www2.minneapolismn.gov/resident-services/property-housing/property-info/landmarks/alphabetical/gluek-building/

Oldest Improv Company: Email correspondence with Dale Stark; "The Singular Life of Dudley Riggs." *MinnPost.* Sept. 24, 2020;" An Oral History of Dudley Riggs' Brave New Workshop." *Star Tribune.* Sept. 22, 2020; https://bravenewworkshop.com/theatre-history/; "My North—Episode 49: Dudley Riggs, Jan. 10, 2018

Oldest Basilica in the Nation: Email correspondences with Heather Craig and Shannon Luckert; Numerous site visits; R. L. Cartwright. "Basilica of St. Mary, Minneapolis." *MNopedia*, MNHS; Larry Millett. 2007. *AIA Guide to the Twin Cities: The Essential Source on the Architecture of Minneapolis and St. Paul.* pp. 86-87. MNHS Press; www.mary.org/who-we-are/our-history/parish-history; https://www.ncregister.com/features/americas-oldest-basilica

Oldest Nicollet Mall Art: https://nicolletmallart.org/; "Restoring a Nicollet Mall Landmark." Kare 11 News. June 1, 2017; "Bringing the Nicollet Mall Sculpture Clock Back to Life." https://www.legacy.mn.gov/projects/historic-nicollet-mall-sculpture-clock-conservation; CBS Minnesota. Sept. 21, 2017

Oldest "Best Bar": Site visit Nov. 5, 2021; Email correspondence with Toni Zaccardi; "Palmer's Bar Selling to Longtime Grumpy's NE Bartender Tony Zaccardi," *The Growler*, April 7, 2018; "Inside Minneapolis's Palmer's Bar, Where Bonnie Raitt Was Once a Regular," *The Current,* July 24, 2019; "Palmer's Bar Changes Hands: What's Next for the Iconic Spot?" *Mpls.St.Paul Magazine,* May 7, 2018; "Minneapolis Hangout Named One of 'Best Bars in America,"*Star Tribune.* May 28, 2014; Bill Lindeke and Andy Sturdevant. Closing Time. MNHS. 2019. pp. 137–142

Oldest American Indian Center: Site visit May 2, 2022; Email correspondences with Jack Auginash and Laura Lablanc; Gatherings Cafe Puts Indigenous Foods at the Forefront. Kare 11 News. Oct. 3, 2020; http://www.maicnet.org/; https://www.minneapolis.org/cultural-districts/districts/franklin-avenue-east/; "Minneapolis American Indian Center Affirms Its Place in the Neighborhood with Huge Renovation." *InForum,* June 7, 2022; "Plans in Works to Expand/Upgrade Minneapolis American Indian Center." *The Circle News.* March 4, 2018; https://www.nacdi.org/cultural-corridor; "In Minneapolis, a Thriving Center for Indigenous Art." *New York Times.* Oct.

20, 2021; "Native American Cultural Corridor Helps Rejuvenate E. Franklin in Minneapolis." *Star Tribune.* Nov. 3, 2019; https://alleynews.org/2016/04/for-the-native-youth-of-phillips-there-are-a-lot-of-possibilities-out-there-to-be-a-part-of/

Oldest Library: Site visit Sept. 29, 2021; Email correspondence with Joshua Yetman; "1834 Emerson Avenue North: North Branch Library." Oak Highland Neighborhood Association. *Minneapolis Historical*; "The Oldest Library in Minneapolis Returns to Life," MPR, May 6, 2005; https://streets.mn/2014/11/13/franklin-library-celebrates-100-years-of-service/; http://www.placeography.org/index.php/

Oldest Washburn-Fair Oaks Mansion: "Eugene Merrill House on Washburn Fair Oaks Park." *Forgotten Minnesota.* May 19, 2020; "Washburn Fair Oaks." *Mill City Times.* March 10, 2019; https://www.bigboytravel.com/minnesota/minneapolis/washburn-fair-oaks-mansions/; https://www.minneapolisparks.org/parks-destinations/parks-lakes/washburn_fair_oaks_park

Oldest Food Co-op: Site visit Sept. 20, 2022; Email correspondence with Karah Barr; *The Co-op Wars,* Deacon Warner. 2021; Craig Cox. *Storefront Revolution: Food Co-ops and the Counterculture.* Rutgers University Press.1994; "The Oldest Co-op in Town." *The Minnesota Daily.* Feb. 25, 2016; http://www2.mnhs.org/library/findaids/; "The Seward Friendship Store Sparks Return of the Co-op War." *Twin Cities Daily Planet.* July 10, 2015; "Q&A with Angela Dawson, 40 Acre Co-op." *Minnesota Women's Press.* Oct. 27, 2021; "A Brief Fascinating History of Food Coops in the Twin Cities." *Star Tribune.* Oct. 24, 2019; "New Documentary Looks at the Booming '70s Twin Cities Food Co-op Scene — and How It Almost Fell Apart." *Pioneer Press.* May 15, 2021; The Co-op Wars Documenting the Fall and Rise of Minnesotas Flower Power Co-ops. *Co-op News.* June 5, 2021

Oldest Sci-Fi Bookstore: Site visit and impromptu interview with Don Blyly Sept. 7, 2022; www.unclesstoriesproject.weebly.com; "Bookmark the Return of the Uncles and Other Good News." *Star Tribune.* Aug. 22, 2022. "Uncle Hugo's Science Fiction Bookstore Attacked, Burned to the Ground in Minneapolis Riots." SCIFI.radio. May 31, 2020

Oldest Hiking Trail: Site visit May 13, 2021; Walk and Talk Self-guided Tour Brochure; https://mntrips.com/winchell-trail-minneapolis/; https://serc.carleton.edu/vignettes/collection/25473.html; https://www.esci.umn.edu/winchell; https://en.wikipedia.org/wiki/Winchell_Trail

Oldest Preservation: Site visit May 10, 2022; https://www.minnesotahistory.org/post/the-day-10-000-minneapolis-children-moved-a-house; "Moving the Stevens House." *Nokohaha.* Nov. 16, 2018; "May 29, 1896: Schoolchildren Move a House." *Star Tribune.* Aug. 15, 2015; https://hennepinhistory.org/moving-the-stevens-house/; https://www.minneapolisparks.org/parks-destinations/historical_sites/john_h_stevens_house/; "History

Hiding in Plain Sight," *Minneapolis Star Tribune Magazine*, Summer 2021; "Discover the Hidden House in Minnehaha Park where Minneapolis Was Born." *Star Tribune.* June 22, 2021; http://www.johnhstevenshouse.org/about.html; https://collections.mnhs.org/; https://www.fox9.com/news/historic-stevens-house-in-minneapolis-catches-fire-for-third-time-since-august

Oldest Cemetery: Site visit July 19, 2022; Email Correspondence with Susan Weir; Paul Nelson. "Pioneers and Soldiers Memorial Cemetery, Minneapolis." *MNopedia,* Minnesota Historical Society; "Black History Unearthed in Mpls' Oldest Cemetery." *Minnesota Spokesman-Recorder.* Oct. 11, 2018. www.Friendsofthecemetery.org; https://www.theclio.com/entry/97084; "Minneapolis Pioneers and Soldiers Memorial Cemetery and the anti-slavery movement: the Laymans Legacy." *Genealogy Wise.* Oct. 14, 2012; "The Pioneers and Soldiers Memorial Cemetery." *Mill City Times.* June 2, 2021; "Tales from Pioneer and Soldiers Memorial Cemetery." *The Alley Newspaper.* Sept. 12, 2022; "Once Far from the City, an Old Cemetery on Busy Lake Street Hosts Some Famous Minnesotans." *Star Tribune.* June 23, 2020

Oldest Nordic Center: Site visit May 2, 2022; Email correspondence with Julie Ingebretsen; "Minneapolis Stalwart Ingebretsen's Nurtures the Next Generation." *Star Tribune.* Nov. 22, 2021; "A Walkabout History of Lake Street." *Southwest Journal.* Oct. 15, 2012; "How Ingebretsen's Became a 101-Year-Old Scandinavian Institution." *MSP Magazine.* Feb. 24, 2022; https://www.placeography.org/;https://www.ingebretsens.com/

Oldest Bowling Alley: Site visit May 2, 2022; Email correspondence with Erica Gilbert; https://www.bryantlakebowl.com/about; "Bryant-Lake Bowl, a Lyn-Lake landmark, is Changing Hands." *Star Tribune.* Oct. 24, 2018; "Kim Bartmann is Selling Restaurant/Theater/Bowling Alley Concept Bryant-Lake Bowl." *MSP Business Journal.* Oct. 23, 2018

Oldest Black-Owned Business: Site visit June 30, 2022; Email correspondence with Tracey Williards-Dillard; "From the Magazine: Spokesman for the Community." Hennepin History Museum. Fall 2010, Vol. 69, No. 3; "'Super cool': Minnesota's Oldest Black-owned Newspaper Puts Its Archive Online." *MPR News.* May 30, 2021; "Chauvin Trial Cuts Close to Home for State's Oldest Black-owned Newspaper and Founding Family." Kare 11 News. April 21, 2021; "Minnesota Spokesman-Recorder: Celebrating 85 Years in Hennepin Gallery through February 28." *Mill City Times.* Feb. 4, 2020; Tina Burnside. "Southside African American Community, Minneapolis;" https://smallbusinessrevolution.org/small-business-revolution/main-street/season-six/episode-1-minnesota-spokesman-recorder; *MNopedia,* MNHS

Oldest Rose Garden: Numerous site visits; https://hennepinhistory.org/heffelfinger-fountain/; https://minnevangelist.com/lyndale-park-gardens-minneapolis-minnesota/; www.minneapolisparks.

org/parks; http://www.eastharriet.org/heffelfinger-fountain.html

Oldest State Building: Several site visits; Email correspondence with Bill Convery; Sarah Shirey. "Round Tower, Fort Snelling." *MNopedia,* Minnesota Historica Society; "Fort Snelling: From Military Post to Historic Site. *Minnesota History.* Dec. 1956. pp. 178-192; "Round Tower at Fort Snelling was a 'Lovely Home' to Grow Up In." *Star Tribune.* Aug. 1, 2015; https://openrivers.lib.umn.edu/article/fort-snelling-as-i-knew-it/Society; https://www.usdakotawar.org/river-stories; https://www.mnhs.org/fortsnelling/learn/transcript; http://treatiesmatter.org/; https://bdote.wordpress.com/; https://www.tclf.org/places/view-city-and-regional-guides/twin-cities/twin-cities-landscape-legacy; https://www.usdakotawar.org/history/treaties/minnesota-treaties; Fort Snelling at Bdote.National Trust for Historic Preservation; https://www.fortsnelling.org/

Oldest Natural Spring: Site visits May 10, 2022 and Aug. 14, 2022; Email correspondences with Bruce White, Bill Convery, and Eden Bart; https://bdotememorymap.org/learn-more/; https://www.fortsnelling.org/post/why-save-coldwater-spring; http://friendsofcoldwater.org/history/birthplace/birthplace.html; https://sacred-sites.org/susu-jeffrey-coldwater-springs-minnesota/; https://www.minnesotahistory.net/; https://www.nps.gov/places/coldwater-spring.htm

Oldest Jewish Deli: Site visit May 10, 22; Email correspondence with Becca Kvasnik; "Restaurants Come and Go, but Cecil's Deli in St. Paul Has Lasted Since 1949." *Star Tribune.* Feb. 18, 2019; https://heavytable.com/great-twin-cities-pastrami-tour/; "St. Paul's Cecil's Delicatessen Marks 70 Years of Serving Up Matzo Ball Soup, Pastrami Sandwiches and More." *Pioneer Press.* June 27, 2019

Oldest Golf Course: Site visit with Rick Wilhoit, July 20, 2022; https://www.tcc-club.com/about; "Town & Country Club." *Nokohaha.* Oct. 31, 2021; John Husar. "How 1st Golf Links Evolved in Minnesota." *Chicago Tribune.* Feb. 19,1969; "An Insider's Guide to Twin Cities Private Country Clubs." *Artful Living.* May 27, 2013; https://archive.lib.msu.edu/tic/holen/article/2004nov25.pdf; https://archive.lib.msu.edu/tic/holen/article/2002nov14.pdf

Oldest Carousel: Many site visits; Email correspondence with Tamara Beckley; https://www.ourfaircarousel.org/history/; "Gerard Cafesjian Helped Save Carousel" (obituary). *Pioneer Press.* Oct. 2, 2013; "Cafesjian Carousel: Going Round and Round Since 1914." *Pioneer Press.* July 23, 2014

Oldest State Fair Ride: Email correspondences with Minnesota State Fair Archive volunteers; https://www.mnstatefair.org/get-involved/media/history; "State Fair Buys Ye Old Mill from Founder's Descendants." MPR News. Jan. 15, 2018; "As Renovated Ye Old Mill Readies for State Fair Action, Ex-Owners Look Forward to Just Enjoying the Fair." *MinnPost.* Aug. 22, 2018;"Ye Old Mill Marks 100 Years at State Fair." *Park Bugle.* Sept. 17, 2022

Oldest University: Site visit April 8, 2022; Email correspondence with Jeff Papas; Frederick Johnson. "Origins of Hamline University." *MNopedia*, MNHS; https://www.hamline.edu/about/mission-history/history; "Hamline's Old Main." *Nokohaha.* July 27, 2012; "Old Main Hall at Hamline University." *Historic Twin Cities.* July 27, 2018. Johnson, David W. *Hamline University, A history.* North Central Press. 1980

Oldest Park Shelter: Site visit July 15, 2022; Paul Nelson. "Wigington, Clarence (1883–1967)." *MNopedia*, MNHS; "Mosaic on a Stick Tessellates a Good Story." *Midway Como Frogtown Monitor.* May 8, 2017; "The Outsized Architectural Legacy of Clarence Wigington." National Trust for Historic Preservation. Savingplaces.org. Nov. 2, 2016

Oldest Used Bookstore: Site visit and impromptu interviews with owners April 22, 2022; https://discoverthecities.com/midway-used-rare-books-photo-tour/; "Midway Rare and Used Books Celebrates 50 years." *Midway Como Frogtown Monitor.* Tuesday, June 9, 2015

Oldest Black Church: Email correspondence with Nate Galloway; Tina Burnside. "African Americans in Minnesota." *MNopedia*, MNHS; "Pastor of Oldest Black Baptist Church in Minnesota Reflects on Using Faith to Strengthen the Past and Present." *CBS Minnesota.* Nov. 25, 2020. "Pilgrim Baptist Church, Founded by Former Slaves, Celebrates 150 Years." MPR News. June 13, 2013; *Storied: The Pilgrims.* MNHS; https://www.blackpast.org/african-american-history/pilgrim-baptist-church-saint-paul-minnesota-1863/

Oldest Synagogue: Weber, Laura. "From Exclusion to Integration: The Story of Jews in Minnesota." *MNopedia*, MNHS; https://mountzionhistory.wordpress.com/; https://mzion.org/about/history/our-history/; "Letter by Letter, a Torah is Born." *Pioneer Press.* May 25, 2007/Updated Nov. 14, 2015

Oldest "New" Supper Club: Site visit Oct. 1, 2022; Email correspondence with Josh Thoma; "The Lexington Rises." *MSP Magazine.* Feb. 22, 2017; "The Lexington is Back Baby." *MSP Magazine.* April 24, 2017; "Why the Lexington Once Mattered, Still Matters, Will Matter for Years to Come." *Twin Cities Agenda.* Feb. 9, 2018; "St. Paul's 'The Lexington' Brings a Storied History to the Modern Age." *The Hungry Minnesotan.* YouTube. Nov. 14, 2019; "St. Paul's Lexington Has a New Chef in Charge. *Star Tribune.* Nov. 17, 2021; "'A Giant in Every Way': Chef Jack Riebel Has Died." *CBS Minnesota.* Dec. 7, 2021

Oldest Curling Roots: Site tour with Scott Clasen, July 15, 2022; Eric Weber. "St. Paul Curling Club." *MNopedia*, MNHS; "160 Years of Curling in Minnesota." *The Growler.* Jan. 22, 2016; https://saintpaulhistorical.com/; "St. Paul Curling Club Marks 100 years on Selby Avenue." *Pioneer Press.* Dec. 22, 2012; "The St. Paul Curling Club Longtime Home of Good Play Serves Curlers Near and Far." www.lisastories.com. Nov. 26, 2019

Oldest Outdoor Sculpture: Numerous site visits; https://publicspaces.guide/; "Rescue and Restoration of St. Paul's First Outdoor Sculpture, Icon of Its Past." *Ramsey County History Magazine.* Vol. 37, No. 3. Fall 2002; "The Survival of Outdoor Sculpture in St. Paul." *Ramsey County History Magazine.* Vol 46, No. 3, Fall 2011; "New York Life Eagle – Historic St. Paul Sculpture is Reborn." *Star Tribune.* April 30, 1999; http://publicartstpaul.org/wp-content/uploads/2015/06/Sculptures-of-Summit-Avenue.pdf

Oldest Czech-Slovak Hall: Site visit with Joan Sedlacek July 15, 2022; www.sokolmn.org; R. L. Cartwright. "St. Paul Sokol." *MNopedia*, MNHS; "Sokol Keeps Czech-Slovak Heritage Alive." MPR News. April 2, 2008; Riehle, Dave. "Czech and Slovak Workers." *St. Paul Historical*; https://saintpaulhistorical.com/items/show/246

Oldest Lager Saloon: Email correspondence with Tom Schroeder; Site visit May 11, 2022; https://waldmannbrewery.com/; Bill Lindeke and Andy Sturdevant. *Closing Time: Saloons, Taverns, Dives, and Watering Holes of the Twin Cities.* MNHS Press. 2019. pp. 11-16. "Secrets of the Stone House." *Star Tribune.* Nov. 30, 2010; "The German Lager Saloon Could be Making a Comeback in St. Paul." *Pioneer Press.* July 19, 2014; https://www.rewire.org/historic-waldmann-brewery/; "Renovation of St. Paul's Oldest Commercial Structure Nears the Finish Line." *Star Tribune.* Aug 7, 2015; "Historic Waldmann Brewery Celebrates America's Past and Present." TPT Originals. Dec. 11, 2018

Oldest Firehouse: Site visit Oct. 8, 2021; Email correspondence with Gates Lindquist; "Breakfast Bar Going into St. Paul's Oldest Fire Station." *Pioneer Press.* Aug. 2, 2019; https://www.stpaulrealestateblog.com/2019/04/historic-firehouse.html; https://www.historicsaintpaul.org/projects/hope-engine-co-no-3; https://www.purposerestaurants.com/

Oldest Neighborhood (St. Paul): Many site visits; "Irvine Park in 1854: "Its Homes and the People Who Once Lived There 150 Years Ago." *Ramsey County History Magazine.* Spring 2004. Vol. 39, No. 1; "This Historic 'It' Neighborhood Was Nearly Destroyed." TPT Originals. Jan. 27, 2020; "Preservation Before the Preservationists: The Beginning of Preservation in St. Paul." *Ramsey County History Magazine.* Summer 2001. Vol. 36, No. 2; "Set in Stone: "Exploring St. Paul's Oldest Neighborhood." PBS Originals. Season 2, Episode 15. March 23, 2020

Oldest Italian Market: Site visit April 9, 2022; Email correspondence with Wesley Just; "Photos of the Famous (and not): Distinctive Decor on St. Paul's West Seventh." *MinnPost.* Aug. 8, 2012; "Cossetta's Quietly Opened a Casual Italian Street Food Restaurant." *Minnesota Monthly.* March 17, 2021; https://www.bonappetit.com/story/comfort-minnesota-cossetta/amp; "Cossettas A St Paul Classic Grows Thanks to Owners Vision. *Pioneer Press.* Jan. 15, 2013; "Cossetta's Alimentari: An Italian Market & Pizzeria in St. Paul, MN." *Histastrophe!* July 22, 2019

Oldest Cultural Institution: Site visit April 22, 2022; Email correspondences with Bill Convery and Ann Regan; https://www.mnhs.org/historycenter/; https://www.mnhs.org/about/history; https://youtu.be/lCeceBEp53s

Oldest Public Square: "St. Paul's Rice Park is 170 Years Old. Here's its History in Photos." *Pioneer Press.* May 19, 2019; "St. Paul's Rice Park Blooms Anew After $2.3M Makeover." *Star Tribune.* June 12, 2019; https://streets.mn/2018/08/03/the-story-of-rice-park; https://www.saintpaulparksconservancy.org/rice-park-revitalization/; https://www.planning.org/greatplaces/spaces/2011/ricepark.htm

Oldest Downtown Building: Site visit with owner Mary Arvanitis Sept. 16, 2022; "The Original Coney Island Cafe and Tavern." *St. Paul Historical;* "St. Paul's Original Coney Island Restaurant Opening Saturday—For One Day Only." *Star Tribune.* Feb. 2, 2017; "Original Coney Island, St. Paul MN - Jason Davis." *On the Road.* 1986

Oldest Railcar Diner: Site visits through the years; John Fitzgerald. "Mickey's Diner." *MNopedia,* MNHS. "Mickey's and Al's: What's Happening with the Twin Cities' Two Most Iconic Diners?" *MinnPost.* April 1, 2021; "Downtown St. Paul Finds a Way Forward as Pandemic Drags On." *Star Tribune.* July 9, 2022; "Mickey's Diner—Everybody Knows Mickey's." www.lisastories.com. June 6, 2019

Oldest Art Museum: Site visit May 11, 2022. Email correspondences with Kate Beane and Ann Benrud; "Minnesota Museum of American Art Debuts New Space, Exhibitions in December." Artwire Press Release from ArtfixDaily.com. Nov. 25, 2018; https://www.aia-mn.org/minnesota-museum-of-american-art/; https://mmaa.org/; "Minnesota Museum of American Art is Homeless No Longer." *Star Tribune.* Nov. 27, 2018; "The Comeback: MN Museum of American Art." TPT Originals. Nov. 15, 2018; "Welcome to the New, Old Minnesota Museum of American Art." *Minnesota Monthly,* Nov. 20, 2018

Oldest Theater Space: Email correspondence with Ashley Ryan. "F. Scott Fitzgerald Society events open to the public." *MinnPost.* June 27, 2017; https://first-avenue.com/venue/the-fitzgerald-theater/; http://cinematreasures.org/theaters/; "First Ave. to Buy Fitzgerald Theater from MPR." MPR News. Oct. 24, 2018; "100-Year-Old Fitzgerald Theater Makes National Register." MPR News. Sept. 17, 2010; "First Avenue Inks Deal with MPR to Acquire St. Paul's Fitzgerald Theatre." *Twin Cities Business.* Oct. 24, 2018; First Avenue Buying Spree Continues With Deal for MPR's Fitzgerald Theater. *Star Tribune.* Oct. 25, 2018

Oldest Sporting Club: Site visit July 23, 2021; Email correspondence with Charlie Stockwell; https://www.minnesotaboatclub.org/; Sarah Risser. "Minnesota Boat Club, 1870–1900." *MNopedia,* MNHS. "Upholding the Amateur Ideal at the Minnesota Boat Club." *Ramsey County History Magazine.* Ramsey County Historical Society. Summer 2018. Vol 53. No. 2.; Minnesota Boat Club Still Rowing After 151 Years. *Star Tribune.* Aug.

8, 2021; St. Paul Summer Fun: Row Classes Teach Adventure, Teamwork on the River. *Pioneer Press.* Oct. 28, 2015; St. Paul's Restored Raspberry Island Praised. *Pioneer Press.* Nov. 14, 2015; "Raspberry Island the Little Island That Could." www.lisastories.com. Sept. 15, 2018

Oldest Mexican Eatery: Site visit April 9, 2022; Email correspondence with owner Jose Frías; https://www.bocachicarestaurant.com/our-story/;Obituary: Gloria Frías, Founder of Boca Chica Restaurant. *Star Tribune.* Jan. 9, 2016; "Boca Chica's 'Freddie' Frías, Helped Bring Mexican Culture to St. Paul's West Side, Dies at 63." *Pioneer Press.* April 25, 2018; Paul Nelson."District del Sol." *St. Paul Historical;* "Boca Chica Celebrates 50 Years." *Lake Minnetonka Magazine*

Oldest Cited Cave: Site visit June 8, 2022; Email correspondences with Ben Gessner and Maggie Lorenz of the Lower Phalen Creek Project; https://www.lowerphalencreek.org/bruce-vento-nature-sanctuary; "On Language and Legacy: Wakáŋ Tipi." *The Circle.* Feb. 4, 2021; "Sacred in the City: Indigenous Site in St. Paul Prepared to Welcome, Educate Public." *MPR News Northstar Journey.* June 14, 2022; "After 184 Years, a Home for Dakota People and Culture Returns to Wakan Tipi." *MinnPost.* Oct. 28, 2021; "Wakan Tipi Dakota Sacred Land." YouTube. Nov. 11, 2020; Steve Trimble. "Is it Carver's Cave or Wakan Tipi?" *St. Paul Historical;* https://saintpaulhistorical.com/items/show/8

Oldest Brewery Reborn: Site visit with Thomas Keim June 8, 2022; https://www.yoergbeer.com; "History Glass: Yoerg Brewing Co. is on a Mission to Bring the Wealth of Old-World Beer to Minnesota Through an Impressive Import Tap List." *The Growler.* April 3, 2020; "Yoerg Beer—Then and Now." *Minnesota Good Age.* June 28, 2019; Doug Hoverson. *Land of Amber Waters: The History of Brewing in Minnesota.* University of Minnesota Press, 2007. pp. 287

Oldest Family Italian Restaurant: Site visit June 8, 2022; Email correspondence with Mike and Annette Yarusso; Nels M. Hokanson. "I remember St. Paul's Swede Hollow." *MN History Magazine.* pp. 362-371; Matt Reicher. "Swede Hollow." *MNopedia,* MNHS; "Swede Hollow Sheltered Immigrants as They Began Pursuit of American Dream." *Pioneer Press.* May 12,1999; Steve Trimble. "Yarusso Brothers Italian Restaurant," *St. Paul Historical;* https://www.yarussos.com/about.html

Oldest Roundhouse: Site visit April 9, 2022; Email correspondences with Barb Sheldon; "Everybody Loves to Ride the Train': It's Grand Central Station at Minnesota Transportation Museum." CBS Minnesota. April 6, 2022; Paul Nelson. "Hill, James J. (1838–1916)." *MNopedia,* MNHS; https://transportationmuseum.org/train-rides/roundhouse-museum/

Oldest Cemetery: Site visit July 23, 2021; Email correspondence with Bob Schoenrock; Oakland Cemetery Self-guided Tour Brochure; Paul Nelson. "Oakland Cemetery, St. Paul." *MNopedia,* MNHS;

https://oaklandcemeterymn.com/map/mastermap.
asp; "St. Paul's Forgotten Cemetery." *Forgotten Minnesota*. May 23, 2012

Oldest Pro Theater: Numerous site visits; Email correspondence with Maureen Kvam; Bob Aden. *The Way It Was: A Highly Personal Account of the Old Log Theatre's Early Years*, edited by Linda I. Higgins, Old Log Theatre, 1989; "Old Log Theater Endures in Its Neck of the Woods." *MinnPost*. MNHS. April 21, 2008. "Don Stolz, Twin Cities Theater Legend, Dies at 97." *Star Tribune*. Feb. 17, 2015; "Old Log Theatre in Minnesota Is Sold." *Star Tribune*. Feb. 15, 2015

Oldest Dugout Canoe: West Hennepin History Center visit Dec. 3, 2022; "New Tests Confirm Lake Minnetonka Canoe Is 1,000 Years Old." Star Tribune. April 11, 2014; "Historic Canoe Gets Spotlight." Southwest News Media. April 11, 2014; https://northernwilds.com/strange-tales-the-ancient-dugout-canoe/; https://hennepinhistory.org/from-the-magazine-native-dugout-canoes/

Oldest Magic Shop: Site visit and interview with Larry Kahlow May 18, 2022; "The Ultimate Trickster." Murphy News Service. April 1, 2014; "Eagle Magic Offers a Shop Full of Tricks."*Star Tribune*. March 31, 2015; "The Oldest Joke Shop in the U.S. Is Right Here in Minnesota — and It's Still Going Strong." *The Minnesota Daily*. March 28, 2017; https://shopdinelive.net/2021/07/06/eagle-magic-store/; https://www.davidfarr.com/minneapolis-has-the-oldest-magic-shop-in-the-u-s/

Oldest Music Store: Site visit Aug. 20, 2021; Interview with Melanie Peterson, Jan. 12, 2022; Email correspondences with Todd Johnson; https://www.grothmusic.com/t-gjallarhorn.aspx; https://www.vikings.com/fans/gjallarhorn; "Groth Music's Todd (TJ) Johnson Creates the Gjallarhorn for the Minnesota Vikings." YouTube. Jan. 30, 2012

Oldest Suburb: Site visit to Richfield History Center on May 18, 2022. Email correspondence with Jon Wickett; http://www.richfieldhistory.org/; "Richfield, the State's 'Oldest Suburb.'" *Star Tribune*. Feb. 11, 2008; "Richfield, Once the Land of Rich Buttermilk." *Star Tribune*. Feb. 19, 2008; https://www.mnhs.org/mgg/boom/suburbia/learn-more; "Richfield a Classic Minnesota Postwar Suburb." YouTube. Jan. 19, 2009

Oldest Private Home: Site visits June 18 and Sept. 12, 2022; Email correspondences with Bill Convery and Jack Nord; Peter DeCarlo. "US–Dakota War of 1862." *MNopedia*. MNHS; Rhoda Gilman. "Sibley, Henry H. (1811–1891)." *MNpedia*, MNHS; http://www.usdakotawar.org; Peter DeCarlo. "Fort Snelling at Bdote: A Brief History." MNHS Press, 2017; "The Mount Vernon of Minnesota: The Sibley House." *American Spirit*. Jan./Feb. 2012; https://www.dakotahistory.org/sibley-historic-site; https://redhawksonline.com/2018/04/20/bdo-te-mdo-te-mendota-reflecting-on-where-the-rivers-come-together/; "Partnership Gives New Life to the Home of Minnesota's First Governor." *Star Tribune*. May

22, 2016; http://www.sibley-friends.org/; Curt Brown. Six-part series 150th Anniversary Tribute US Dakota War. *Star Tribune*. Aug. 12–17, 2012

Oldest Church in the State: Exterior site visits June 18 and Sept. 12, 2022; Email correspondence with Julie Bardon; Reverend John T. Bauer Pastor. *A History of St. Peter's Church, Mendota, MN* – Published on the occasion of the dedication of our new place of worship October 1974; 150th Anniversary Booklet *The History of St. Peter's Catholic Church* – Mendota, MN 1840-1990; https://www.dakotahistory.org/images/HistoryMaps/Mendota-History-Map.pdf

Oldest BluffTop Landmark: Site visit Sept. 12, 2022; Email correspondences with Bruce White and Eden Bart; http://pilotknobpreservation.org/; http://treatiesmatter.org/treaties/land/1851-Dakota; "Oȟéyawahe (Pilot Knob): A Teacher Guide and Supplementary Lessons for Learning about Mnísota's First People." Minnesota Humanities Center. 2019; https://www.dakotahistory.org/historical-sites/140-pilot-knob

Oldest Grain Elevator: Site visit Aug. 11, 2022; https://slphistory.org/nordicware/; https://www.nordicware.com/history-behind-the-iconic-nordic-ware-tower/; "Sculptor Goes with the Grain in St. Louis Park Project." *Star Tribune*. May 14, 2013

Oldest Lilac Way Relics: Site visits Aug. 11 and Sept. 19, 2022; Email correspondences with Karen Laukkonen and Andrea Weber; www.restorelilacway.com; "Picking Up Pieces of Past from Area Roads, Highways." *Star Tribune*. Oct. 7, 2008; ''Lilac Drive" - Twin Cities PBS Documentary. Sept. 26, 2001; https://homesmsp.com/2019/05/when-highway-100-was-called-lilac-way.html

Oldest Public Wildflower Garden: Several site visits. "Botanist Eloise Butler left a living legacy at Theodore Wirth Regional Park." *Star Tribune*. April 27, 2019; "Eloise Butler Continues Teaching Minneapolis Kids Nearly 80 Years After Her Death." *MinnPost*. MNHS. June 7, 2012; https://www.minneapolisparks.org/; "Get to Know the Gilded-Age Visionaries Who Dreamed Up Minneapolis' Parks." TPT Originals. May 18, 2020; http://www2.mnhs.org/library/findaids/00384.xml; https://www.friendsofthewildflowergarden.org/pages/eloisebutler.html

Oldest Bar in State: Site visit May 26, 2022; North St. Paul Historic Walking Tour Guide brochure; "Minnesota's Oldest bar? North St. Paul's Neumann's Claims the Title." *Pioneer Press*. Aug. 12, 2016; "Step Inside Neumann's Bar: MN's Oldest, Continually Active Watering Hole." Twin Cities PBS Originals. July 19, 2019; "Finding Minnesota: State's Oldest Bar, 1 Year Later." CBS News. Dec. 29, 2013

Oldest Skate Shop: Site visit with staff May 26, 2022. Molly Huber. "Strauss Ice Skates." *MNopedia*, MNHS; "Strauss Skates Is Probably the Oldest Hockey Shop in the U.S." *Mpls.St.Paul Magazine*.

Feb. 11, 2021; https://www.shopstrauss.com/ info/history; http://www2.mnhs.org/library/ findaids/00463.xml

Oldest Lutheran Church: Site visit June 2, 2022; Email correspondence with Lynne Moratzka; https://gammelgardenmuseum.org/; Joy Lintelman."Swedish Immigration to Minnesota." *MNopedia*, MNHS; https://wildwomenwanderers. wordpress.com/2013/07/14/gammel-garden-museum-scandia-minnesota

Oldest General Store: Site visit June 2, 2022; Email correspondence with Gwen Roden; "'Ralph's Pretty Good Grocery.'"*Country Messenger*. June 5, 2020; "Marine on St. Croix's General Store Nears Rare Change of Hands." *Star Tribune*. March 31, 2015

Oldest Courthouse: Site visit Sept. 18, 2021. Email correspondence with Elise Gardner; Dunn, James Taylor. "Minnesota's Oldest Courthouse." *Minnesota History*, vol. 38, no. 4, 1962, pp. 186–189; https:// www.co.washington.mn.us/; "Washington County Historic Courthouse." *Historic Twin Cities*. Aug. 30, 2019

Oldest Ice Cream Shop: Site visit July 2, 2022; Email correspondence with Rebecca Nickerson; "Selma's Ice Cream Looking for a Buyer." *Star Tribune*. March 2, 2011; "Houlton Family Purchases Selma's in Afton." *Republican Eagle*. Nov. 13, 2011; "Selma's Ice Cream Parlour to Reopen in Afton in Spring." *Pioneer Press*. Nov. 15, 2011; "Ice Cream Shop Throws Open Its Doors." *Republican Eagle*. April 25, 2012; "Summers Without Selma's Ice Cream 'Won't Be the Same,' Afton Mayor Says." *Pioneer Press*. Nov. 12, 2015

Oldest Winery: Site visit July 2, 2022; Email correspondence with Nan Bailly; "Nan Bailly Guides Alexis Bailly Vineyard." *Midwest Wine Press*. April 4, 2012; https://www.thewinecompany.net/mn-connection-alexis-bailly/

Oldest Hotel: Email correspondence with Rebecca Shaw. "Landmarks: Anderson House: Wabasha." *Minnesota History Magazine*. Winter 2015-16. pp. 307; https://www.theandersonhousehotel.com; "The Wabasha Wander." *Minnesota Monthly*. Aug. 2, 2017; "Cat-filled Haunted Hotel Still on the Market." *Winona Daily News*. Feb. 11, 2009; "Anderson House, Minnesota's Oldest Hotel, Closes." *Star Tribune*. March 23, 2009; Anderson House: Nostalgia for the Soul and a Cat for the Bed." *Chicago Tribune*, Sept. 29, 1985; Wabasha Couple Buys Anderson House. *LaCrosse Tribune*. Nov. 26, 2011; Landmark Wabasha Hotel May Reopen Next Year. *LaCrosse Tribune*. Jan. 27, 2021

Oldest Covered Bridge: "Zumbrota: The First 100 Years-1856-1956." Zumbro Valley Historical Society, 1956; Email correspondence with city administrator Brian Grudem; Email correspondence with Bill Caswell, President, National Society for the Preservation of Covered Bridges; "Bridges of Goodhue County." *Mpls.St.Paul Magazine*. Sept. 1, 2021; City of Zumbrota 2021 Visitors' Guide; "Step Back in Time Inside the State's Oldest Covered Bridge." TPT Originals. Aug. 6, 2019; https:// www.dot.state.mn.us/historicbridges/25580. html#features; https://ancestralfindings.com/the-history-of-covered-bridges-in-america/

Oldest Observatory: Email correspondences with Trenne Fields and Cindy Blaha; Molly Huber. "Goodsell Observatory, Northfield." *MNopedia*, MNHS; Andy Sturdevant. "Checking out Carleton's Goodsell Observatory — and Its Fascinating History." *MinnPost*. April 17, 2015; https://www. carleton.edu/goodsell/history/story-of-goodsell/

Oldest Wool Mill: Email correspondence with Ann Sviggum. Peter DeCarlo. "Faribault Woolen Mill Company." *MNopedia*, MNHS; https://www. faribaultmill.com/blogs/the-thread/the-mill; https:// visit-twincities.com/hit-the-road/stories/behind-scenes-faribault-woolen-mill-co/; "2 Businesses That Lived Through US History Show American Traditions." *ABC News*. Dec. 11, 2020

Oldest Continuous Brewery: Site visit in previous years; Email correspondence with Johnny Germscheid; https://www.schellsbrewery.com/our-story/; "Schell Brewery Buys Grain Belt Beer Sign, Land." *The Journal*. Feb. 2, 2016; "Schell's to Light the Grain Belt Sign with Ceremony Tonight." *The Journal*. Dec. 30, 2017; "Marti Details How Schell's Survived Prohibition." *The Journal*. Oct. 4, 2019; "Still All in the Family: Next Generation of Martis Stepping Up to Run August Schell Brewery." *The Journal*. Feb. 25, 2021; Minnesota Legacy Brands: August Schell Brewing Company. *Minnesota Monthly*. Jan. 25, 2022

Oldest Savu Sauna: Email correspondence with Heidi Barberg of the Cokato Finnish-American Historical Society; https://www.cokatofinnamhs. org/; Molly Huber. "Barberg-Selvälä-Salmonson Sauna, Cokato." *MNopedia*, MNHS; "Book on Finnish Sauna Traditions Features Cokato's Historical Savusauna." *Herald Journal*. Dec. 20, 2010; https://gallery.lib.umn.edu/exhibits/show/ juhla--celebrating-150-years-o/sauna; Michael Nordskog. "*The Opposite of Cold: The Northwoods Finnish Sauna Tradition*." Cokato Finnish-American Historical Society 2010. pp. 8-15

INDEX

Alexis Bailly Vineyard, 162–163, 182
Anderson House, 164–165, 182
Arvanitis, Mary, 105, 180
Arvanitis, Nicholas, 104–105
Aster Cafe, 8
August Schell Brewing Company, 172, 182
Bailly, Alexis, 138, 162–163
Bailly, David, 162–163
Bailly, Nan, 163, 182
Bartholomew House, 137
Bartmann, Kim, 54, 178
Basilica of St. Mary, 30–31, 177
Bdote, 62, 65, 178
Bishop, Harriet, 81, 125
Blyly, Don, 44–45, 177
Boca Chica, 114–115, 180
Brave New Workshop, 18, 177
Bryant Lake Bowl, 54–55, 177
Bureau of Mines, 65
Cafesjian's Carousel, 70–71, 178
Capri, 4–5, 176
Carleton College, 168
Carver's Cave, 116, 180
Cecil's Deli, 66–67, 178
Cedar Riverside, 34
Cheatham, John W., 51
City House, 61
Cleveland, Horace W. S., 125
Coldwater Spring, 64–65, 178
Como Park, 70–71, 76
Cossetta, 97–99, 179–180
Countryman, Gratia, 39
C.S.P.S. Hall, 90–91
Dakota, vi, 6, 14, 31, 46, 62–65, 80, 96, 116,
    137–139, 142–143, 172–173, 178, 180
Depot, The, 16–17, 176
Dinkytown, 6
Eagle Magic Store, 132–133, 181
Eat Street, 41
Eloise Butler Wildflower Garden, 148
Faribault Mill, 170
Finnish-American Historical Society, 175,
    182
First Bridge Park, 20–21
Fitzgerald, F. Scott, 103, 110, 180
Fitzgerald Theater, 110, 180
Floyd, George, 35, 44, 56
Forepaugh, Joseph, 96
Fort Snelling, 6, 49, 62–65, 80, 99, 136–
    137, 141–142, 178
Franklin Avenue East Cultural District, 36
Franklin Library, 38–39
Frías, Freddie, 115
Galtier, Father Lucien, 140–141
Gammelgården Museum, 154–155, 182
General Mills, 18, 41
Gilbert, Cass, 69
Gilbert, Erica, 55
Gjallarhorn, 134–135, 181

Glickman, Cecil and Faye, 66–67
Gluek's, 22, 26–27
Godfrey, Ard, 6, 11–13, 176
Goodridge, William C.
Goodsell Observatory, 51
Graeser Park, 146–147
Grand Avenue, 84
Great Northern Railway, 122
Green, Lori, 77
Groth Music, 134, 181
Guthrie Theater, 19
Halprin, Lawrence, 32
Hamline-Midway, 74, 76, 79
Hamline Park, 76
Hamline University, 74–75, 179
Hamm's, 150
Heffelfinger Fountain, 59, 178
Hennepin, Father Louis, 31, 176
Hennepin Avenue, 9, 20, 25, 31
Hennepin County Library System, v
Hennepin History Magazine, 50, 57
Hennepin History Museum, v, 41, 178
Hennepin Theatre Trust, 29
Hickman, Robert T., 80–81
Hidden Falls Regional Park, 67
High Bridge, 61, 89, 91–92
Hill, James J., 1, 69, 122
Historic Anderson House Hotel, 164–165,
    182
Historic Church of St. Peter, 140
Historic Fort Snelling, 62–63
Hoćokata Ti, 131
Hope Breakfast Bar, 94–95
Hopkins Mainstreet, 127
Indian Mounds Regional Park, 117
Ingebretsen's, 52–53, 178
Irvine, John, 96, 102
Irvine Park, 96, 102, 179
Island Sash and Door Company, 14–15
Jackson Street Roundhouse, 122–123
Jax Cafe, 2–3, 176
Kahlow, Larry, 132–133, 181
Keillor, Garrison, 111, 156
Keim, Thomas, 118–119, 180
Lake Minnetonka, 128, 130–131, 180–181
Lake Street, 52–53, 178
Landmark Center, 103, 105
Layman, Martin and Elizabeth, 50, 178
Lexington, The, 84, 179
Lilac Way, 146–147, 181
Loring Greenway, 33
Lower Phalen Creek Project, 117, 180
Lumber Exchange Building, 24–25, 176
Lyndale Park Rose Garden, 58
Main Street Southeast, 6, 8–9
Marcy-Holmes, 6, 176
Marine General Store, 156
Mendota Bridge, 142
Mickey's Diner, 106, 180

Midway Used and Rare Bookstore, 78–79
Mill City Museum, 18–19
Mill Ruins Park, 18–20
Minneapolis American Indian Center, 36–37
Minneapolis Institute of Arts, 40–41
Minneapolis Woman's Club, 13
Minnesota Boat Club, 112, 180
Minnesota Historical Society, v, 19, 33, 57, 62, 89, 93, 96, 100–101, 138, 178
Minnesota History Center, 100–101
Minnesota Museum of American Art, 108, 180
Minnesota Spokesman-Recorder, 56–57, 178
Minnesota State Capitol, 69, 100–101, 124
Minnesota Transportation Museum, 122
Minnesota Vikings, 134–135, 181
Mississippi River, 1, 6, 14, 18, 20, 24, 32, 46, 48, 61–62, 68, 80–82, 86, 112, 118, 138, 164
Mní Ówe Sní, 64–65
Monte Carlo, 22, 176
Mosaic on a Stick, 77, 179
Mount Zion Temple, 82–83
National Eagle Center, 165
National Register of Historic Places, 17, 38, 50, 117, 127, 142, 164, 167, 171
Neumann's Bar, 150–151, 181
Newman, Cecil Earle, 56
Newman, Launa Q., 57
New York Life Eagle, 88, 179
Nicollet Island, 14, 21, 27, 172, 176
Nicollet Mall, 32–33, 177
Nordic Ware, 144–145, 181
Northeast Minneapolis, 3, 8, 15, 27
Northloop, 22–23, 176
North Minneapolis, 4–5, 176
Oakland Cemetery, 124–125, 181
Ohage, Justus, 96
Oȟéyawahe, 142–143, 181
Old Log Theatre, 128–129, 181
Ordway, Lucius Pond, 69
Original Coney Island, 104–105, 180
Our Lady of Lourdes Church, 10–11
Overlook Park, 88–89
Palmer's Bar, 34, 177
Peavey-Haglin Experimental Elevator, 144–145
Peavey Plaza, 32
Pike, Zebulon, 6, 62
Pike Treaty, 6, 62
Pilgrim Baptist Church, 80–81, 179
Pillsbury A Mill, 8
Pilot Knob, 142–143, 181
Pioneer-Endicott Building, 109
Pioneers and Soldiers Memorial Cemetery, 50, 178
Plympton, Joseph, 6
Pracna, 8–9, 176
Prince, 5
Prohibition, 3, 25, 27, 150, 173, 182
Ramsey, Alexander, 96, 119, 125, 139
Raspberry Island, 86, 112–113, 180

Restored Lilac Park, 145–147
Rice Park, 102–103, 180
Richfield History Center, 136–137, 181
Riebel, Jack, 85, 179
Riggs, Dudley, 28–29, 177
Round Tower, 62, 178
Schell Brewing Company, 172–173, 182
Schroeder, Tom, 92–93, 179
Schubert Club, 113
Schulz, Charles, 103
Sculpture Clock, 32
Selma's Ice Cream Parlor, 160–161, 182
Seward Community Co-op, 42–43
Sibley, Henry, 125, 138
Sibley Historic Site, 138–139, 181
Spot Bar, The, 151
St. Anthony Falls, vii, 6, 8, 9, 12, 18, 20–21, 24, 31, 49
St. Paul Curling Club, 86, 179
St. Paul Hotel, 103
St. Paul Winter Carnival, 76, 102–103, 105
State Fair, 70, 72–74, 178
Steele, Franklin, 6, 12, 20, 138
Stevens, John H., 48–49
Stevens House, 48–49, 177–178
Stolz, Don, 129, 181
Stone Arch Bridge, 1, 6, 8, 16, 139
Strauss Skate Shop, 152–153, 182
Summit Avenue, 83, 88–89, 122, 179
Swede Hollow, 120–121, 180
Symonds, Charles, 97
Town & Country Club, 68, 178
Uncle Hugo's Bookstore, 44–45
University of Minnesota, 45–46, 57, 180
Uptown, 28, 54
US-Dakota War of 1862, 63, 80, 139, 172
Vaughn, Oscar, 51
Wakan Tipi, 116–117, 180
Waldmann Brewery, 92–93, 179
Wanáǧi Wíta (Spirit Island), 21
Warehouse District, 22–23
Washburn, Cadwallader, 18, 41
Washburn, William D., 41
Washburn A Mill, 18, 176
Washburn Fair-Oaks Park, 40, 177
Washington County Historic Courthouse
   West Hennepin History Center, 158, 182
West Seventh Street, 99
Weir, Susan, 51, 178
Wigington, Clarence W., 76–77, 179
Williams-Dillard, Tracey, 57
Winchell Trail, 46–47, 177
Wirth, Theodore, 58, 148, 151
Works Progress Administration, 76
XCel Energy Center, 8, 96, 118, 152
Yarusso-Bros, 120
Ye Old Mill, 72–73, 178
Yoerg Brewing Company, 118–119
Zaccardi, Tony, 35, 177
Zumbrota Covered Bridge, 166–167, 182